INSTANT GOURMET EXCITEMENT

Exquisite desserts — thick, rich sauces — frothy, cooling drinks. Of course you'd like to serve your family and guests the best, but you just don't have time to spend hours in the kitchen.

Now learn to cheat in style with the NEW BLENDER COOKBOOK. Shows you how to make complicated cheese sauces in seconds, perfect pâtés in a matter of moments. 200 nonfail recipes provide you with an impressive range of gourmet marvels.

And remember — no one will ever guess it was done instantly, with a blender.

THE NEW BLENDER COOKBOOK

The Only Blender Cookbook for the 2- to 14-Speed Blenders

WILLIAM I. KAUFMAN

PYRAMID BOOKS NEW YORK

THE NEW BLENDER COOKBOOK

A PYRAMID BOOK

First printing, January, 1969

Printed in the United States of America

PYRAMID BOOKS are published by Pyramid Publications, Inc.
444 Madison Avenue, New York, New York 10022, U.S.A.

Table of Contents

Preface

WITH THE ELECTRIC BLENDER in my kitchen I am like Aladdin with his magic lamp, for at the press of my fingertip I bring forth a variety of the most delicious culinary miracles and the real touch of magic lies in the time saving as well as in the taste. The ease and speed with which I can chop vegetables, crush ice for desserts, grind coffee beans, whip up beverages and purée fruits makes it possible for me to provide the reader of *The New Blender Cookbook* with a rainbow of recipes that suit every need, for every meal, from sandwich spreads for the family to party paté that pleases the palate of the most discriminating gourmet guest.

And, now, no recipe is too complicated or too time-consuming. The electric blender has made it possible to prepare everything in one third the time. Sauces and dressings take seconds; foreign specialties are whipped together in minutes and popped into the oven or skillet sooner than it used to take to slice the onions and from the standpoint of nutrition, every vitamin and mineral is preserved. Nothing is lost or needs to be thrown away. The electric blender helps to get full value of food dollars. Delectable concoctions can be made from bits of this and that left over from past culinary efforts.

The electric blender is the 20th-century home-makers' secret weapon against waste, kitchen fatigue and menu boredom. It can be used to add interest and originality to appetizers, main dishes, desserts, beverages and snacks.

Here in this *New Blender Cookbook* are a multitude of recipes that will make you a genie in your own kitchen. The magic lies in your electric blender.

WILLIAM I. KAUFMAN

Spreads and Dips

SHRIMP-CUCUMBER SPREAD

2 tablespoons chili sauce
1 thin wedge lemon, peeled and seeded
Dash Worcestershire sauce
1/4 teaspoon dill seed
1 package (3 ounces) soft cream cheese, cubed
1/4 peeled cucumber, cut up
1 cup (approximately 1 small can) cleaned, cooked shrimp

PLACE chili sauce, lemon, Worcestershire sauce, dill seed and cream cheese in blender container.
COVER AND PROCESS until smooth.
ADD cucumber and shrimp and continue to process until chopped.
STOP BLENDER and scrape down sides of container with rubber spatula, if necessary.
SERVE on caraway rye bread or whole-wheat bread.
MAKES: 6 to 8 sandwiches.

BRAUNSCHWEIGER SPREAD

2 tablespoons pickle juice
1/2 pound Braunschweiger (liver sausage), cubed
1/4 medium onion
1 stalk celery, cut up
1/8 teaspoon Tabasco sauce
2 sprigs parsley

PLACE all ingredients in blender container.
COVER AND PROCESS until smooth.
MAKES: 1-1/2 cups.

CHICKEN SALAD SPREAD

3 tablespoons mayonnaise
1 medium stalk celery, cut in 2-inch pieces
1 teaspoon Worcestershire sauce
1/4 teaspoon salt
1 cup cooked chicken, cubed

PLACE all ingredients except chicken in blender container.
COVER AND PROCESS until smooth.
ADD chicken.
COVER AND PROCESS until chicken is chopped.
STOP BLENDER and scrape down sides of container with rubber spatula, if necessary.
MAKES: 1 cup.

EGG SALAD SPREAD

1/4 cup mayonnaise
1/4 teaspoon salt
1/4 teaspoon onion salt
1/8 teaspoon pepper
1/8 teaspoon paprika
1/2 stalk celery, cut in 2-inch pieces
4 hard-cooked eggs

PLACE all ingredients except eggs in blender container in order listed.
QUARTER eggs and separate whites from yolks.
ADD yolks to blender container.
COVER AND PROCESS until ingredients are chopped.
STOP BLENDER and scrape down sides of container with rubber spatula, if necessary. Add egg whites.
COVER AND PROCESS just until egg whites are coarsely chopped.
MAKES: 1-1/2 cups.

GARLIC BUTTER

1/2 cup soft butter
1 to 2 cloves garlic, quartered

PLACE butter and garlic in blender container.
COVER AND PROCESS at low speed until smooth.
STOP BLENDER and scrape down sides of container with rubber spatula, if necessary.
MAKES: 1/2 cup.

HAM SALAD SPREAD

1/4 cup mayonnaise
1 pickle, cut in 1-inch pieces
1 slice onion
1 cup cooked ham, cubed

PLACE butter and honey in blender container.
COVER AND PROCESS until ham is chopped.
STOP BLENDER and scrape down sides of container with rubber spatula, if necessary.
MAKES: 3 to 4 sandwiches.

HERB BUTTER

1/2 cup soft butter
1 teaspoon lemon juice
3/4 teaspoon thyme, rosemary, basil or tarragon

PLACE all ingredients in blender container.
COVER AND PROCESS at low speed until smooth.
STOP BLENDER and scrape down sides of container with rubber spatula, if necessary.
MAKES: 1/2 cup.

HONEY BUTTER

1/2 cup soft butter
½ cup honey

PLACE all ingredients in blender container.
COVER AND PROCESS at low speed until combined.
STOP BLENDER and scrape down sides of container with rubber spatula, if necessary.
SERVE on hot biscuits, waffles, pancakes etc.
MAKES: 1 cup.

LIVER PATE

2 tablespoons butter
1/2 pound chicken livers
1 medium onion, sliced
1 clove garlic, split
1/4 cup mayonnaise
1 hard-cooked egg, quartered
1 teaspoon lemon juice
1/2 teaspoon salt
1/4 teaspoon pepper

MELT butter over medium heat.
ADD chicken livers.
SAUTE about 5 minutes until tender.
ADD onion and garlic.
COOK 2 minutes over low heat until onion is soft.
PLACE all ingredients in blender container.
COVER and process until smooth.
STOP BLENDER and scrape down sides of container, if necessary.
REFRIGERATE until serving.
MAKES: 1-1/2 cups.

LOBSTER SPREAD

1 cup cooked lobster meat, cubed
1/4 cup mayonnaise
3 hard-cooked eggs

PLACE all ingredients in blender container.
COVER AND PROCESS until smooth.

STOP BLENDER and scrape down sides of container with rubber spatula, if necessary.
MAKES: about 1-1/2 cups.

NUT BUTTER

2 cups salted nuts, almonds, cashews, peanuts, etc.
1 to 2 tablespoons salad oil

PLACE half nuts in blender container.
COVER AND PROCESS to chop nuts.
EMPTY nuts into bowl.
REPEAT procedure with remaining nuts.
PLACE one fourth cup of chopped nuts and one tablespoon salad oil in blender container.
COVER AND PROCESS until mixture is smooth.
REMOVE feeder cap and slowly add remaining nuts. If mixture is very thick and a butter consistency is not reached, a little more salad oil should be added.
STOP BLENDER and scrape down sides of container with rubber spatula, if necessary.
MAKES: 1-1/2 cups.

TUNA SPREAD

1 can (7 ounces) tuna, drained
1/2 cup mayonnaise
1/4 teaspoon prepared mustard
1/2 small onion
2 sprigs parsley
1 3-inch dill pickle, cut in pieces

FLAKE tuna into a medium bowl.
PLACE all ingredients except tuna in blender container.
COVER AND PROCESS until smooth.
POUR over tuna and mix well.
MAKES: 1-1/2 cups.

SHRIMP SOUP DIP

1 can frozen condensed cream of shrimp soup, thawed
1 package (3 ounces) cream cheese, softened and quartered
1 teaspoon lemon juice
1/4 teaspoon garlic powder
Crackers, raw carrot, celery, or cauliflower

PLACE all ingredients in blender container.
COVER AND PROCESS at high speed until smooth.
STOP BLENDER and scrape down sides of container with rubber spatula, if necessary.
CONTINUE PROCESSING.
SERVE as spread for crackers or as dip for raw carrot sticks, celery sticks and cauliflower.
MAKES: about 1-1/2 cups.

GUACAMOLE DIP

1 large ripe avocado
1/2 small onion
1 very small clove garlic
1 stalk celery
1/4 teaspoon Tabasco
1/4 teaspoon salt
1/4 teaspoon mayonnaise
1/2 small hot green pepper
Crackers or potato chips

CUT avocado and celery into 1-inch pieces.
PLACE in blender container.
ADD all the other ingredients.
PROCESS until smooth.
STOP BLENDER and scrape down sides of container with rubber spatula, if necessary.
REMOVE dip from container and serve on crackers or potato chips.
MAKES: 1/2 cup.

BAVARIAN CHIP DIP

- 1 package (3 ounces) cream cheese, softened at room temperature
- 2 tablespoons lemon juice
- 1 package (8 ounces) Braunschweiger (liver sausage)
- 1 envelope dried onion soup mix
- 1 tablespoon prepared horseradish
- 1 teaspoon Worcestershire sauce
- Dash of Tabasco
- 2/3 cup evaporated milk

COMBINE cream cheese and lemon juice in blender container.
COVER AND PROCESS until smooth.
ADD remaining ingredients.
COVER AND PROCESS at high speed until completely blended.
CHILL before serving.
MAKES: approximately 2 cups.

ANCHOVY DIP

- 1/2 cup evaporated milk
- 1/2 cup salad oil
- 1/4 cup wine vinegar
- 1 teaspoon salt
- 1/4 teaspoon pepper
- Dash of garlic powder
- ¼ cup parsley pieces
- 1 can (2 ounces) flat fillets of anchovies
- Crackers or potato chips

PLACE all ingredients in blender container.
COVER AND PROCESS for a few seconds until smooth.
CHILL. Serve with crackers or potato chips.
MAKES: about 1 cup.

AVOCADO DIP

1 ripe avocado, peeled and cubed
1 tablespoon lemon juice
1 thin slice onion
1/8 teaspoon salt
Dash Worcestershire sauce
3 ounces cream cheese, softened and cut in small pieces

PLACE all ingredients except cream cheese in blender container.
COVER AND PROCESS on high speed to purée until smooth. With blender continuing to run,
REMOVE feeder cap and slowly add cream cheese.
COVER AND PROCESS until smooth.
CHILL before serving.
MAKES: 1 cup.

BEAN DIP

1 can (15 ounces) garbanzos, drained
2 tablespoons salad oil
1/4 cup lemon juice
1 teaspoon dried parsley flakes
2 cloves garlic
1/2 teaspoon salt

PLACE all ingredients in blender container.
COVER AND PROCESS to chop until smooth.
STOP BLENDER and scrape down sides of container with rubber spatula, if necessary.
CHILL before serving.
MAKES: 1-1/2 cups.

CHEDDAR CHEESE DIP

2 cups creamed cottage cheese
1/2 teaspoon Worcestershire sauce
1/8 teaspoon garlic salt
1/8 teaspoon onion salt
1 tablespoon mustard
8 ounces Cheddar cheese, cubed

PLACE all ingredients except Cheddar cheese in blender container.
COVER AND PROCESS on high speed until smooth. With blender continuing to run,
REMOVE feeder cap and slowly add Cheddar cheese.
COVER AND PROCESS until smooth.
STOP BLENDER and scrape down sides of container with rubber spatula, if necessary.
CHILL before serving.
MAKES: 2 cups.

DEVILED HAM DIP

1 package (8 ounces) cream cheese, softened
2 tablespoons milk
1 can (4-1/2 ounces) deviled ham
1 teaspoon Worcestershire sauce
1 thin slice onion

PLACE all ingredients in blender container.
COVER AND PROCESS to mix until smooth.
STOP BLENDER and scrape down sides of container with rubber spatula, if necessary.
CHILL before serving.
MAKES: 1 cup.

DIETER'S DIP

1 cup creamed cottage cheese
1/4 cup skim milk
1 teaspoon horseradish
Dash Worcestershire sauce
Dash garlic salt
Dash celery salt
2 radishes, cut in half
1 stalk celery, cut in 2-inch pieces
1 carrot, cut in 2-inch pieces
1/2 green pepper, cut in 2-inch pieces
1/2 medium onion, cut in 2-inch pieces

PLACE cottage cheese, milk, horseradish, Worcestershire sauce, garlic salt and celery salt in blender container.
COVER AND PROCESS to mix until smooth. With blender continuing to run,
REMOVE feeder cap and slowly add remaining ingredients.
COVER AND PROCESS until vegetables are chopped.
CHILL before serving.
MAKES: 1 cup.

NIPPY BLUE CHEESE DIP

1 cup creamed cottage cheese
1/8 teaspoon onion salt (optional)
1/8 teaspoon garlic salt (optional)
4 dashes Worcestershire sauce
2-1/2 ounces blue cheese, crumbled

PLACE first 4 ingredients in blender container.
COVER AND PROCESS until smooth. With blender continuing to run,
REMOVE feeder cap and slowly add blue cheese.
STOP BLENDER and scrape down sides of container with rubber spatula, if necessary.
CONTINUE to process until smooth.
CHILL before serving.
MAKES: 1-1/4 cups.

PINEAPPLE-HAM DIP

3/4 cup pineapple chunks, drained
2 cans (2-1/2 ounces each) deviled ham
1 package (3 ounces) cream cheese, broken into pieces

PLACE all ingredients in blender container in order listed.
COVER AND PROCESS to mix until smooth.
STOP BLENDER and scrape sides with rubber spatula, if necessary.
CHILL before serving.
MAKES: 1-1/2 cups.

QUICK CHIP DIP

2 cups creamed cottage cheese
1/4 cup sour cream
2 teaspoons dry Italian salad-dressing mix

PLACE all ingredients in blender container.
COVER AND PROCESS on high speed until smooth.
STOP BLENDER and scrape down sides with rubber spatula, if necessary.
CHILL before serving.
MAKES: 1-1/2 cups.
VARIATION: Substitute the same amount of dry Parmesan cheese salad dressing, herb salad dressing, garlic salad dressing, etc., for the Italian salad-dressing mix.

SHRIMP DIP

1/2 cup sour cream
1/2 cup mayonnaise
1 package (8 ounces) cream cheese
1/2 onion, cubed
Dash Worcestershire sauce
2 cups cooked, cleaned shrimp

PLACE all ingredients except shrimp in blender container.
COVER AND PROCESS on high speed until smooth.
With blender continuing to run,
REMOVE feeder cap and slowly add shrimp.
COVER AND PROCESS until smooth.
STOP BLENDER and scrape down sides of container with rubber spatula, if necessary.
CHILL before serving.
MAKES: 3-1/2 cups.

SWISS CHEESE DIP

1 cup creamed cottage cheese
1/2 teaspoon Worcestershire sauce
1 teaspoon prepared mustard
1 tablespoon mayonnaise
1 slice onion
1 cup Swiss cheese, cubed

PLACE all ingredients except Swiss cheese in blender container.
COVER AND PROCESS on high speed until smooth.
With blender continuing to run,
REMOVE feeder cap and slowly add Swiss cheese.
COVER AND PROCESS until smooth.
CHILL before serving.
MAKES: 1 cup.

TUNA DIP

- 2 tablespoons milk
- 1/2 teaspoon Worcestershire sauce
- 1-1/2 cups cream style cottage cheese
- Dash salt
- 1 can (7 ounces) tuna
- 1 tablespoon capers
- 1 teaspoon horseradish
- 1/4 teaspoon celery salt
- 1/4 teaspoon garlic salt
- 1/4 teaspoon monosodium glutamate

PLACE ingredients in order listed in blender container.
COVER AND PROCESS on high speed until smooth.
STOP BLENDER and scrape down sides of container with rubber spatula, if necessary.
CHILL before serving.
MAKES: 2 cups.

YULE CHEESE BALL

- 1/2 cup pecans
- 6 sprigs parsley
- 1/4 cup milk
- 1 package (3 ounces) blue cheese, cubed
- 1/4 cup Cheddar cheese, cubed
- 1 small wedge onion
- 1 teaspoon Worcestershire sauce
- 2 packages (3 ounces each) cream cheese, cubed
- Crackers

PLACE pecans and parsley in blender container.
COVER AND PROCESS until coarsely chopped.
REMOVE from container.
PLACE milk and blue cheese in blender container.
COVER AND PROCESS on high speed about 5 seconds. With blender continuing to run,
REMOVE feeder cap and slowly add Cheddar cheese.
Add onion, Worcestershire sauce and cream cheese.

COVER AND PROCESS on high speed until smooth.
STOP BLENDER and scrape down sides of container with rubber spatula, if necessary.
REMOVE from container and shape into a ball.
REFRIGERATE overnight. Roll cheese ball in pecan-parsley mixture before serving on crackers.
MAKES: one 3" ball.

Appetizers

CHEESE-HAM BALLS

1 package (8 ounces) cream cheese, cubed
1 can (4-1/2 ounces) deviled ham
1 cup chopped nuts

PLACE cream cheese and ham in blender container.
COVER AND PROCESS on high speed until smooth.
STOP BLENDER and scrape down sides of container with rubber spatula, if necessary.
REMOVE mixture from container.
CHILL until firm enough to handle.
SHAPE into small balls.
ROLL in chopped nut meats.
SERVE on toothpicks.
MAKES: 2-1/2 dozen.

DEVILED EGGS

6 hard-cooked eggs
1 teaspoon prepared horseradish
1/4 cup mayonnaise
1/2 teaspoon prepared mustard
1/4 cup blue cheese, crumbled (optional)
Parsley bits and paprika for garnish

CUT eggs in half lengthwise.
REMOVE yolks.
PLACE yolks in blender container and add horseradish, mayonnaise, mustard and blue cheese.

COVER AND PROCESS on high speed to mix until well blended.
MOUND MIXTURE into whites.
GARNISH with parsley bits and paprika.
MAKES: 12 deviled eggs.

MOLDED PATE

- 3 tablespoons brandy
- 1 can (3 or 4 ounces) chopped mushrooms
- 1/2 pound chicken livers
- 1 can condensed beef bouillon, divided
- 1 envelope unflavored gelatine
- 1 teaspoon Worcestershire sauce
- 1/2 cup pitted ripe olives
- 1/4 cup parsley leaves
- 1/4 teaspoon nutmeg
- wafers or toast

COMBINE brandy and liquid from mushrooms in small saucepan.
ADD chicken livers.
BRING to a boil.
COOK rapidly until livers are done and liquid has evaporated, about 5 minutes.
POUR 1/4 cup bouillon in blender container.
SPRINKLE gelatine over liquid. Allow to soften.
HEAT 1/2 cup bouillon to a boil.
ADD to blender.
COVER AND PROCESS at proper speed for gelatine (low) until gelatine dissolves. If gelatine granules cling to container, use a rubber spatula to push them into the mixture.
ADD remaining bouillon, mushrooms, chicken livers and other ingredients.
COVER AND PROCESS at high speed until smooth.
POUR into 3-cup mold or 2 small molds.
CHILL until firm, several hours or overnight.
UNMOLD and serve with crisp wafers or toast.
MAKES: 2-1/2 cups.

DELUXE SHRIMP PATE

3 to 4 tablespoons Pernod
Juice of 1/2 lemon
1/2 teaspoon mace
Dash Tabasco
1 teaspoon prepared mustard
1/4 pound butter, softened
Salt and pepper to taste
1 pound shrimp, cooked, shelled
Toast triangles

PLACE all ingredients except shrimp in blender container.
COVER AND PROCESS to blend.
REMOVE feeder cap and add 3 or 4 shrimp at a time until coarsely chopped.
STOP BLENDER and scrape down sides of container with rubber spatula, if necessary.
TURN mixture into mold or bowl and chill.
SERVE with toast triangles.
MAKES: 2 cups.

QUICK PATE

1/2 pound chicken livers
1/4 pound (1 stick) butter
2 ounces cognac
1/2 pound cream cheese, cubed
2 hard-cooked eggs, quartered
Truffles
Toast rounds or crackers

SAUTE chicken liver in about 3-1/2 tablespoons butter and cool.
PLACE livers in blender container with cognac, cream cheese and eggs.
COVER AND PROCESS until smooth. Turn mixture into a bowl.
GARNISH with truffles.
SPREAD with enough melted butter to cover.
REFRIGERATE. Serve on toast rounds or with crackers.
MAKES: 2-1/2 cups.

TARAMA

2/3 cup red caviar
1/4 small onion
4 sprigs parsley
Juice of 1 lemon
2 slices fresh bread, broken in 1-inch pieces
1 cup olive oil
Toast fingers or crackers

PLACE caviar in blender container with onion, parsley and lemon juice.
COVER AND PROCESS only until mixture is smooth.
ADD bread, a little at a time.
THEN ADD olive oil very gradually, adding only enough to make mixture stiff like mayonnaise.
KEEP in refrigerator for about a week.
SERVE with toast fingers or crackers.
MAKES: 1-3/4 cups.

BLUE CHEESE MOLD

1/2 cup cold milk
2 envelopes unflavored gelatine
1 cup milk, heated to boiling
6 ounces blue cheese, cut in pieces
1/2 teaspoon salt
1/4 teaspoon Tabasco
1 shallot, sliced
1 cup parsley leaves
1/4 cup lemon juice
1-1/2 cups heavy cream
Parsley for garnish
Cherry tomatoes for garnish

PLACE cold milk and gelatine in blender container.
COVER AND PROCESS at proper speed for gelatine (low) until gelatine is softened.
REMOVE feeder cap and add boiling milk.
PROCESS until gelatine dissolves. If gelatine granules cling to container, use a rubber spatula to push them into the mixture. When gelatine dissolves,
TURN control to proper speed and liquify remaining ingredients, except garnishes. Turn into 4-cup mold or bowl.
CHILL until firm, 4 hours or over night.

UNMOLD.
GARNISH with parsley and cherry tomatoes.
MAKES: 4 cups.

CURRIED EGG BALLS

1 slice bread, cut in 1-inch pieces
1/4 cup nuts
1/4 cup mayonnaise
6 hard-cooked eggs, quartered
1/4 teaspoon curry powder
1/4 teaspoon salt
Dash of pepper
2 tablespoons butter

PLACE bread and nuts in blender container.
COVER AND PROCESS as for nuts until finely grated. Set aside.
PLACE remaining ingredients, except butter, in blender container.
COVER AND PROCESS until smooth.
SHAPE into 1/2-inch balls.
BROWN crumb mixture in butter.
ROLL egg balls in crumb mixture.
STORE in refrigerator.
MAKES: about 2 dozen balls.

STUFFED CELERY

20 1 1/2-inch pieces of celery
1/4 cup mayonnaise
1 carrot, cut in 1-inch pieces
4 sprigs parsley
2 green olives, pitted
1/8 teaspoon salt
Dash of pepper
Pinch basil

SOAK celery in ice water to make it crisp. Set aside.
PLACE remaining ingredients in blender container.
COVER AND PROCESS on high speed until smooth.
STOP BLENDER and scrape down sides of container with rubber spatula, if necessary.
CONTINUE PROCESSING.
REFRIGERATE until thick.

FILL center of celery with chill mixture.
MAKES: 20 pieces.

CHEF'S APPETIZER

1 can (8 ounces) peas, drained
1 can (10-1/2 ounces) condensed chicken with rice soup
2 sprigs parsley
1 soup can water
1 small onion, cut in half
1/2 cup cooked chicken pieces

PLACE all ingredients into blender container.
COVER AND PROCESS until smooth.
CHILL for 24 hours.
STIR before serving.
MAKES: 4 to 5 servings.

APPETIZER ESCOFFIER

1/2 soup can water
1 small onion, cut in half
12 mint leaves
1 garlic clove
1 cup heavy cream
1 can (11-1/4 ounces) condensed green pea soup

COMBINE water, onion, mint leaves and garlic in blender container.
COVER AND PROCESS until smooth.
ADD SOUP and reprocess.
CHILL 24 hours.
STIR in 1 cup heavy cream.
MAKES: 4 servings.

SEAFOOD APPETIZER MOLD

1/4 cup cold milk
1 envelope unflavored gelatine
2 tablespoons butter
1 teaspoon curry powder
1 small apple, pared, cored and sliced
1 small onion, sliced
1/2 cup water
1/2 teaspoon Worcestershire sauce
1/4 teaspoon Tabasco
1/2 cup mayonnaise
1 cup sour cream
2 tablespoons chutney
1/2 pound (2 cups) lump crab meat, cooked shrimp or lobster, or a combination of above

SPRINKLE gelatine over cold milk in blender container.
COVER AND PROCESS at proper speed for gelatine (low) until gelatine is softened.
MELT butter in saucepan.
ADD curry powder, sliced apple and onion.
COOK over low heat until apple and onion are tender, but not brown.
ADD water to saucepan. Bring to a boil.
REMOVE feeder cap from blender container and add boiling apple-onion mixture.
PROCESS until gelatine dissolves. If gelatine granules cling to side of container, use a rubber spatula to push them into the mixture. When gelatine dissolves,
TURN control to high speed and add remaining ingredients *except* seafood.
PROCESS until smooth.
STOP BLENDER AND ADD seafood.
PROCESS until chopped.
TURN into 3-1/2-cup mold and chill until firm, 4 hours or overnight.
UNMOLD.
MAKES: 3-1/4 cups.

FIESTA "GUACAMOLD"

- 2 envelopes unflavored gelatine
- 1/2 cup cold water
- 1/2 cup boiling water
- 2 large avocados, peeled and cut in pieces
- 2 slices onion
- 3 tablespoons lemon juice
- 1 cup sour cream
- 1-1/2 teaspoon salt
- 1 teaspoon chili powder
- 1/4 teaspoon Tabasco

SPRINKLE gelatine over cold water in blender container. Allow to stand while assembling remaining ingredients.
ADD boiling water.
COVER AND PROCESS at proper speed for gelatine (low) until gelatine dissolves. If gelatine granules cling to the container, use a rubber spatula to push them into the mixture. When gelatine is dissolved,
TURN control to highest speed.
ADD remaining ingredients and continue to process until smooth.
TURN into 4-cup mold or bowl and chill until firm, about 4 hours or overnight.
SERVE as appetizer or as salad accompaniment.
MAKES: 8 servings.

DEVILISH EGG TREAT

- 1/4 cup cold water
- 1 envelope unflavored gelatine
- 1/2 cup boiling water
- 1/2 cup mayonnaise
- 3/4 teaspoon salt
- 1/4 teaspoon Tabasco
- 1/4 green pepper, cut in pieces
- 1 cup celery pieces
- 4 hard-cooked eggs, quartered
- Tomato wedges for garnish
- Salad greens

PLACE cold water and gelatine in blender container.
COVER AND PROCESS at proper speed for gelatine (low) until gelatine is softened.
REMOVE feeder cap from blender container.

ADD boiling water and continue to process until gelatine dissolves. If gelatine granules cling to container, use a rubber spatula to push them into the mixture.
REMOVE cover and add mayonnaise, salt and Tabasco.
PROCESS until smooth.
STOP BLENDER AND ADD green pepper, celery and eggs.
COVER AND PROCESS until chopped.
TURN into 3-cup mold or bowl.
CHILL until firm, about 3 hours.
GARNISH with tomato wedges and salad greens, if desired.
MAKES: 4 to 6 servings.

Soups

LA BONNE SOUPE AU POULET

1-1/2 cups cooked chicken or turkey, divided
2 cups chicken broth
1 small onion, chopped fine
3 tablespoons butter
2 tablespoons parsley
1 teaspoon fresh tarragon leaves or 1/3 teaspoon dried tarragon
1 cup heavy cream (cold)
Finely cut parsley for garnish

PLACE 1 cup fine-cut white meat and broth in blender container.
COVER AND PROCESS to blend thoroughly.
SAUTE onion in butter, then add to blender container with rest of chicken, parsley, and tarragon.
COVER AND PROCESS to blend thoroughly.
CHILL.
ADD cream.
CHILL again just before serving.
GARNISH with finely cut parsley and chives.
MAKES: 4 servings.

CREAM OF CARROT SOUP

2 cups carrot pieces
1 onion, quartered
1-1/2 cups milk
1 cup chicken broth
1/3 cup butter
1/2 cup water
2 whole cloves
2 tablespoons flour
1/2 cup cream

PLACE carrots and onions with milk and chicken stock in blender container.

COVER AND PROCESS to chop.
DRAIN through sieve and reserve liquid.
SAUTE vegetables in butter.
ADD water and cloves and cook until tender.
REMOVE cloves and put half reserved liquid, vegetables and butter and flour in blender container.
COVER AND PROCESS until smooth. Pour into saucepan. Add remaining half of reserved liquid and cook slowly about 10 minutes, stirring constantly.
JUST before serving add cream and season to taste.
MAKES: 4 servings.

GREEN PEPPER MEAT SOUP

- 2 large green peppers, cut in pieces
- 1 large onion, diced
- 2 cups canned tomatoes
- 2 slices half-cooked bacon, diced
- 1 quart meat stock or consommé
- Salt and pepper to taste
- 1 pound hamburger

PLACE first 4 ingredients in blender container.
COVER AND PROCESS until vegetables are chopped.
POUR into saucepan with remaining ingredients.
COVER and bring soup to a boil.
SIMMER 1 hour.
MAKES: 6 servings.
Note: To prepare in advance: Cool soup thoroughly, pour into freezing cartons and freeze quickly.

GAZPACHO

Ingredients

2 cans (10-1/2 ounces each) condensed tomato soup
1 to 2 cloves garlic
1 medium onion, sliced
1 small green pepper, seeded and cut in pieces
1 soup can water
2 cups tomato juice
Dash black pepper
Tabasco

Garnishes

1 cucumber, seeded (cut in half lengthwise and scrape out seeds with spoon)
1 green pepper, seeded
1 onion
3 celery stalks
1 ripe tomato
Croutons cooked in garlic butter

PLACE one can of soup in blender container with garlic, onion and pepper.
COVER AND PROCESS to purée.
COMBINE in bowl with remaining soup, water and tomato juice.
SEASON to taste with pepper and Tabasco.
CHILL thoroughly.
SERVE each guest a bowl of soup garnished with vegetables which have been chopped fine and chilled.
MAKES: 6 servings.

WHITE MOUNTAIN REFRESHER

1 can (10-1/2 ounces) frozen condensed cream of potato soup
1 soup can water
1/2 cup sour cream
1/4 cup finely chopped cucumber

COMBINE soup and water in saucepan.
COOK over low heat until soup is thawed.
STIR now and then.
PLACE in blender container.
COVER AND PROCESS until smooth.

STIR in sour cream and cucumber and reprocess.
CHILL in refrigerator at least 4 hours.
SERVE in chilled bowls.
MAKES: 3 servings.

SAVORY CHILLED MUSHROOM BOWL

1 can (10-1/2 ounces) condensed cream of mushroom soup
1 soup can milk
1 teaspoon minced chives or chopped fresh dill
Sour cream, if desired

PLACE soup, milk and seasoning in blender container.
COVER AND PROCESS until smooth.
CHILL at least 4 hours.
SERVE in chilled bowls.
GARNISH with dollop of sour cream, if desired.
MAKES: 3 servings.

VICHYSSOISE

1 can (10-1/4 ounces) frozen condensed cream of potato soup
1/2 soup can milk
1/2 soup can light cream
Garnishes

PLACE soup, milk and cream in saucepan and cook over low heat until soup is completely thawed.
STIR now and then.
PLACE in blender container.
COVER AND PROCESS until smooth.
CHILL in refrigerator for at least 4 hours before serving.
SERVE in chilled bowls.
GARNISH with any of the following: minced chives, minced green pepper, minced parsley, shredded process or grated Parmesan cheese, shredded beets, sliced stuffed olives, minced celery, thinly sliced radishes, chopped cucumber or shredded carrot.
MAKES: 3 servings.

PINK VICHYSSOISE

- 1 can (10-1/4 ounces) frozen condensed cream of potato soup, thawed
- 1/2 soup can light cream
- 1 cup chilled tomato juice

PLACE soup, cream, and tomato juice in blender container.
COVER AND PROCESS until smooth.
SERVE immediately in chilled bowls.
MAKES: 3 to 4 servings.

ENCORE SOUP

- 1 can (1 pound) cut green beans
- 1/4 cup butter or margarine
- 1 cup sliced fresh mushrooms
- 1 tablespoon flour
- 1/2 teaspoon salt
- 1/4 teaspoon tarragon
- 1/8 teaspoon basil
- 1/8 teaspoon white pepper
- Few dashes dry mustard
- 1 cup milk

PLACE beans and liquid in blender container.
COVER AND PROCESS as for vegetables until smooth.
MELT butter in large saucepan.
ADD mushrooms and sauté until tender.
REMOVE from pan with slotted spoon.
BLEND flour, salt, tarrogon, basil, white pepper and mustard into butter in saucepan.
MIX in bean purée and milk.
COOK over low heat, stirring constantly, until mixture comes to boil and is slightly thickened.
ADD mushrooms.
SERVE.
MAKES: 4 to 6 servings.

BROCCOLI CHEESE SOUP

1 package (10 ounces) frozen broccoli
1/2 cup boiling water
1 teaspoon salt
4 tablespoons butter or margarine
1/4 cup finely minced onion
3 tablespoons flour
1 quart milk
1 cup shredded American cheese
1/8 teaspoon pepper
Additional shredded cheese for garnish

COOK broccoli according to package directions in water and salt.
PLACE broccoli and liquid in blender container.
COVER AND PROCESS to purée.
SET ASIDE.
MEANWHILE, MELT butter in saucepan.
ADD onion and sauté until tender.
BLEND in flour.
ADD milk, stirring constantly.
COOK AND STIR until sauce is smooth and thickened.
ADD cheese, pepper and broccoli purée.
STIR until cheese is melted.
SERVE hot.
GARNISH with shreds of cheese.
MAKES: 6 servings.

CLAM CORN CHOWDER

1 can (8 ounces) kernel corn
1 can (7 ounces) minced clams
1 can (10-1/2 ounces) condensed cream of celery soup
1 soup can milk
2 tablespoons butter
Dash black pepper
1 tablespoon bourbon
Croutons

PLACE corn, clams (including liquid) and soup in blender container.

COVER AND PROCESS until smooth.
POUR into saucepan.
ADD milk, butter and pepper.
HEAT slowly until butter is melted and soup is hot.
ADD bourbon.
SERVE with croutons.
MAKES: 4 to 5 servings.

GREEN PEPPER CREAM

- 2 tablespoons butter or margarine
- 1 medium green pepper, chopped
- 1/2 small onion, chopped
- 1 can (10-1/2 ounces) condensed cream of celery soup
- 1 soup can milk

MELT butter in skillet.
PLACE green pepper and onion in skillet.
COOK 5 minutes.
PLACE mixture in blender container.
ADD soup and milk.
COVER AND PROCESS until smooth.
TURN into saucepan.
COOK over low heat, stirring constantly, until heated through.
MAKES: 3 servings.

CHILLED MINTED PEA SOUP

- 1 can (11-1/4 ounces) condensed green pea soup
- 1 soup can milk
- 1/4 cup light cream
- 1/2 teaspoon dried mint flakes, crushed

PLACE all ingredients in blender container.
COVER AND PROCESS until smooth.
CHILL at least 4 hours before serving.
MAKES: 3 to 4 servings.

CUCUMBER COOLER

1 can (10-1/2 ounces) condensed cream of celery soup
1 cup milk
1 small cucumber (about 1 cup), diced
Dash tabasco
Dash salt and pepper
1 cup sour cream

PLACE soup, milk, cucumber, tabasco and seasonings in blender container.
COVER AND PROCESS 2 minutes.
STIR in sour cream.
CHILL in refrigerator for at least 4 hours.
SERVE in chilled bowls.
MAKES: 4 servings.

DANISH FRUIT SOUP
(Sodsuppe)

1 cup dried prunes, pitted
2 cups dried apricots
1 apple, cored and quartered
1/2 cup sugar
1 quart water
1 stick cinnamon
1 cup orange juice
1 tablespoon cornstarch

COOK first six ingredients over low heat until fruits are tender.
REMOVE cinnamon.
COOL.
COMBINE small amount of orange juice with cornstarch.
MIX to smooth paste.
PLACE cornstarch paste, remaining orange juice and cooled fruit mixture into blender container.
COVER AND PROCESS on high speed until smooth.
POUR into saucepan.
COOK, stirring occasionally, until clear.
CHILL thoroughly.
SERVE in chilled soup dishes.
MAKES: 6 to 8 servings.

FROSTY TOMATO SOUP

2 cans (10-1/2 ounces each) tomato soup
Dash garlic salt
1 cup sour cream
1/2 cup cold water
8-10 ice cubes
Chopped chives for garnish

PLACE all ingredients except ice cubes and chopped chives in blender container.
COVER AND PROCESS to liquefy until smooth. With blender continuing to run,
REMOVE feeder cap and slowly add ice cubes.
COVER AND PROCESS until smooth.
POUR into chilled mugs.
GARNISH with chopped chives.
MAKES: 4 to 6 servings.

CREAMED PEA SOUP

1 package (10 ounces) frozen green peas, thawed
2 chicken bouillon cubes
1 thin slice onion
3 tablespoons flour
3 cups milk
Dash pepper
Dash mace

PLACE all ingredients in blender container.
COVER AND PROCESS on high speed until smooth.
POUR into saucepan.
COOK over low heat, stirring constantly.
ADD additional milk if a thinner soup is desired.
MAKES: 6 servings.
VARIATION: Substitute a 10-ounce package of frozen corn for the peas and make creamed corn soup.

CREAM OF MUSHROOM SOUP

1/2 pound fresh mushrooms, cleaned and halved
1 medium onion, quartered
Water
1/4 cup butter
1/4 cup flour
1/2 teaspoon salt
1/4 teaspoon pepper
Dash nutmeg
2 cans chicken broth
1 cup light cream

PLACE mushrooms and onion in blender container.
FILL container to within one to two inches of top with water.
COVER AND PROCESS until finely chopped.
DRAIN in colander or sieve.
MELT butter in heavy saucepan over low heat.
ADD mushrooms and onion.
SAUTE about 10 minutes until tender.
STIR in flour and seasonings until smooth.
SLOWLY ADD chicken broth.
INCREASE temperature and bring mixture to a boil, stirring constantly.
REDUCE heat.
COVER AND SIMMER 5 to 10 minutes.
ADD cream.
COVER AND REHEAT slowly.
MAKES: 6 to 8 servings.

BORSCHT

1 can condensed beef bouillon
1 tablespoon lemon juice
1/2 teaspoon salt
Dash pepper
1/2 teaspoon onion salt
1/2 teaspoon garlic salt
2 cup cooked or canned beets, sliced or diced
6-8 ice cubes
Sour cream for garnish

PLACE all ingredients except ice cubes and sour cream in blender container.
COVER AND PROCESS on high speed until smooth.
With blender continuing to run,

REMOVE feeder cap and slowly add ice cubes until smooth.
POUR mixture into a bowl.
COVER AND REFRIGERATE several hours or overnight.
SERVE COLD in chilled cups.
GARNISH with a spoonful of sour cream.
MAKES: 4 to 6 servings.

Salads

FROZEN PEACH AND PECAN SALAD

1 cup heavy cream
1 cup mayonnaise
2 packages (3 ounces each) cream cheese, cubed
1 cup pecans
8 peach halves

BLENDER-WHIP cream.
EMPTY into large bowl and reserve.
PLACE mayonnaise in blender container.
COVER AND PROCESS to blend.
REMOVE feeder cap and gradually add cheese.
COVER AND CONTINUE PROCESSING until smooth.
ADD pecans.
COVER AND PROCESS to chop (only a few seconds).
FOLD the blended mixture into the whipped cream.
ARRANGE peach halves, hollow side up, in refrigerator tray.
POUR cheese and cream mixture over peach halves.
COVER tightly with aluminum foil and freeze until firm.
THAW before serving.
MAKES: 8 servings.

SUNSHINE SLIM

- 1 envelope unflavored gelatine
- 1/4 cup cold orange juice
- 3/4 cup boiling orange juice
- Non-caloric sweetener equal to 1/4 cup sugar
- 1/8 teaspoon salt
- 1 lemon, peeled and seeded
- 1 cup carrot pieces
- 1 can (8-1/2 ounces) dietetic pineapple (chunks or crushed)

SPRINKLE gelatine over 1/4 cup cold orange juice in blender container.
ADD boiling orange juice.
COVER AND PROCESS at proper speed for gelatine (low) until gelatine dissolves.
ADD non-caloric sweetener, salt and lemon.
PROCESS until lemon is liquefied.
ADD carrot pieces.
COVER AND PROCESS until carrots are chopped.
TURN into bowl.
ADD pineapple and syrup.
CHILL, stirring occasionally, until slightly thickened.
TURN into 3-cup mold.
CHILL until firm, several hours or overnight.
UNMOLD.
SERVE with salad greens and cottage cheese.
MAKES: 6 servings, 90 calories each.

DELTA SUNSET MOLD

2 envelopes unflavored gelatine
1/4 teaspoon salt
1-1/2 cup (12 ounces) regular or low-calorie orange soda, divided
2 fresh Bartlett pears, pared, cored and cubed
1 tablespoon lemon juice
1 cup plain yoghurt
1 tablespoon grated orange rind
Salad greens
Additional pear slices for garnish

COMBINE, gelatine, salt and 1/2 cup soda in top of a double boiler.
PLACE over hot water and stir until dissolved.
COOL slightly.
COAT pear cubes with lemon juice.
PLACE pears in blender container with 1 cup soda and yoghurt.
COVER AND PROCESS until smooth.
FOLD in gelatine mixture and orange rind.
TURN into 4-cup mold.
CHILL until firm.
UNMOLD onto serving plate.
GARNISH with greens and additional pear slices, if desired.
MAKES: 5 servings.

APPLE AND RUTABAGA SALAD

1/2 cup salad oil
1/2 cup evaporated milk
3 tablespoons vinegar
1/2 teaspoon salt
1/4 teaspoon rosemary
Dash of pepper
3 tablespoons sugar
2 cups unpeeled chopped apple
2 cups shredded rutabaga

COMBINE all ingredients except apple and rutabaga in blender container.
COVER AND PROCESS a few seconds until dressing is creamy and smooth.

POUR over apple and rutabaga.
MIX lightly and chill.
SERVE on lettuce.
MAKES: 6 servings.

PATIO COLESLAW

2 envelopes unflavored gelatine
1/2 cup cold water
1 cup boiling water
1 teaspoon salt
2 tablespoons lemon juice
1 cup salad dressing
1 medium onion, quartered
2 cups cabbage pieces
1 cup celery pieces
1 cup cucumber pieces (peeled)
1 can (4 ounces) pimiento, drained and diced
Cherry tomatoes for garnish

SPRINKLE gelatine over cold water in blender container. Allow to stand while assembling remaining ingredients.
ADD boiling water.
COVER AND PROCESS at proper speed for gelatine (low) until gelatine dissolves. If gelatine granules cling to the sides of the container, use a rubber spatula to push them into the mixture. When gelatine is dissolved,
ADD salt, lemon juice and salad dressing.
CONTINUE TO PROCESS until well blended.
STOP BLENDER and add onion.
COVER AND PROCESS until finely chopped.
STOP BLENDER AND ADD cabbage, celery and cucumber pieces.
COVER AND PROCESS only until all pieces are coarsely chopped.
CHILL until mixture is slightly thickened.
STIR in diced pimiento.
TURN into 6-cup mold.
CHILL until firm.
UNMOLD.
GARNISH with cherry tomatoes.
MAKES: 8 servings.

CARROT CAROUSEL

2 envelopes unflavored gelatine
1-1/2 cups cold orange juice divided
1/2 cup boiling orange juice
1/4 teaspoon salt
1 cup salad dressing
1-1/2 cups carrot pieces
1-2/3 cup (13-1/2-ounce can) crushed pineapple, undrained
Watercress and carrot curls for garnish

SPRINKLE gelatine over 1/2 cup cold orange juice in blender container. Allow to stand while assembling remaining ingredients.
ADD boiling orange juice.
COVER AND PROCESS at proper speed for gelatine (low) until gelatine dissolves. If gelatine granules cling to the sides of the container, use a rubber spatula to push them into the mixture. When gelatine is dissolved, ADD remaining 1 cup cold orange juice, salt and salad dressing.
PROCESS until well blended.
STOP BLENDER AND ADD carrot pieces.
COVER AND PROCESS as for raw vegetables until carrots are finely grated.
STIR in pineapple and syrup.
TURN into 6-cup mold.
CHILL until firm.
UNMOLD.
GARNISH with watercress and carrot curls.
MAKES: 8 servings.

PERFECTION SALAD

1/2 cup cold water
2 envelopes unflavored gelatine
1 cup boiling water
1/2 cup sugar
1 teaspoon salt
1/2 cup vinegar
2 tablespoons lemon juice
1 cup crushed ice
2-1/2 cups sliced cabbage
2-1/2 cups celery pieces
1/4 green pepper, cut in pieces
2 pimientos, diced
Tomato slices for garnish
Salad greens for garnish

PLACE cold water and gelatine into blender container.
COVER AND PROCESS at proper speed for gelatine (low) until gelatine is softened.
REMOVE feeder cap from blender container.
ADD boiling water and continue to process until gelatine dissolves. If gelatine granules cling to container, use a rubber spatula to push them into the mixture.
REMOVE cover and add sugar, salt, vinegar and lemon juice.
TURN control as for ice cubes and add ice.
CONTINUE TO PROCESS until ice is melted.
STOP BLENDER AND ADD cabbage, celery and green pepper.
COVER AND PROCESS until chopped.
CHILL mixture until it is the consistency of unbeaten egg white and chopped vegetables stay dispersed throughout the mixture.
FOLD in pimiento and turn into individual molds, 4-cup mold or serving bowl.
CHILL until firm, 2 or 3 hours.
UNMOLD.
SERVE on tomato slices and garnish with salad greens, if desired.
MAKES: 4 to 6 servings.

CABBAGE SALAD

- 1 medium head cabbage (approximately 6 cups)
- 1/2 medium green pepper, cut in 2-inch pieces
- 1/2 medium onion, cut in 2-inch pieces

QUARTER cabbage, wash and remove core. Cut quarters in half lengthwise, then in half crosswise.
PLACE part of cabbage, onion and green pepper loosely in blender container until container is three-fourths full.
FILL container to within one to two inches of top with cold water.
COVER AND PROCESS until vegetables are chopped.
DRAIN in colander to remove water.
PLACE in large bowl.
REPEAT procedure until all vegetables are chopped.
TOSS lightly with Creamy Slaw Dressing or Mayonnaise Slaw Dressing.
REFRIGERATE about one hour to blend flavors.
MAKES: 8 servings.

CREAMY CUCUMBER MOLD

- 1 package (3 ounces) lime-flavored gelatin
- 1/2 cup hot water
- 1 cup mayonnaise
- 1 cup sour cream
- 1 tablespoon lemon juice
- 1/4 teaspoon salt
- 1 medium unpared cucumber, cut in 2-inch pieces
- 1/2 medium onion, quartered

PLACE gelatin and hot water in blender container.
COVER AND PROCESS at proper speed for gelatin (low) until gelatin dissolves.
ADD mayonnaise, sour cream, lemon juice and salt.
COVER AND PROCESS until smooth. With blender continuing to run,

REMOVE feeder cap from lid, and slowly add cucumber and onion.
COVER AND PROCESS until finely chopped.
TURN into 3-cup mold.
CHILL until firm.
MAKES: 4 to 6 servings.

MOLDED VEGETABLE SALAD

1 cup hot water
1 package mixed vegetable flavored gelatin
1 cup mayonnaise
1-1/2 cups finely chopped cabbage
1/2 cup finely chopped green pepper
1/2 cup finely chopped carrots
1/4 cup chopped pecans

PLACE water and gelatin in blender container.
COVER AND PROCESS at proper speed for gelatin (low) until gelatin dissolves.
ADD mayonnaise.
COVER AND PROCESS until smooth.
COOL.
ADD chopped vegetables and pecans to gelatin mixture.
TURN into 1-1/2-quart mold.
CHILL until firm.
MAKES: 4 to 6 servings.

QUICK ORANGE MOLD

1 cup hot water
1 package (3 ounces) orange-pineapple flavored gelatin
Juice from crushed pineapple
1 can (1 pound 4-1/2 ounces) crushed pineapple, drained
4 medium carrots, cut in 1-inch pieces

PLACE hot water and gelatin in blender container.
COVER AND PROCESS at proper speed for gelatin (low) until gelatin dissolves. With blender continuing to run,

REMOVE feeder cap and slowly add pineapple juice.
INCREASE speed to high and slowly add carrots to mixture.
COVER AND PROCESS until carrots are finely chopped.
STOP BLENDER.
FOLD in crushed pineapple.
TURN into a 1-1/2-quart mold.
CHILL until firm.
MAKES: 4 to 6 servings.

Vegetables and Pasta

ASPARAGUS AU GRATIN

2 packages (10 ounces each) frozen asparagus
2 slices white bread
2/3 cup instant dry milk
1/3 cup grated Parmesan cheese, divided
3/4 teaspoon salt
1/2 teaspoon Angostura bitters
1-3/4 cup boiling water, divided
1/4 cup soft butter
1 egg yolk
2 cans (6-1/2 ounces each) crab meat

Preheat oven to 400° F.
COOK asparagus according to package directions.
DRAIN and arrange in shallow baking dish.
BREAK one slice bread in blender container.
COVER AND PROCESS to crumb.
ADD dry milk solids, one half of Parmesan cheese, salt, bitters and about 1/2 cup of boiling water.
COVER AND BEGIN PROCESSING. While processing,
ADD remaining water, bread, butter and egg yolk.
COVER AND PROCESS until smooth.
BREAK crab meat into pieces in large bowl, taking out any cartilage that is present.
POUR sauce over crab meat and stir.
POUR mixture over asparagus.
SPRINKLE with remaining one half Parmesan cheese.
BAKE about 15 minutes or until mixture is bubbly and top browns.
MAKES: 6 servings.

VEGETABLE POTATO SALAD

- 6 cold, cooked potatoes, thinly sliced
- 1 head lettuce, cut in long thin strips
- 2 medium-sized beets, cooked and cut in strips
- Salt and pepper to taste
- 1/4 cup salad oil
- 1/2 teaspoon dry mustard
- 2 tablespoons vinegar
- 1/4 cup sour cream
- 2 egg yolks
- 2 teaspoons sugar

MIX all vegetables lightly in salad bowl.
PLACE remaining ingredients in blender container.
COVER AND PROCESS until smooth.
POUR over vegetables.
TOSS lightly before serving.
MAKES: 4 servings.

POTATO KUGEL

- 4 cups cubed potatoes
- 3 eggs
- 1 large onion, quartered
- 1-1/2 teaspoons salt
- 1/4 teaspoon pepper
- 1/4 cup melted chicken fat
- 1/3 cup potato flour
- 6 sprigs parsley (stems removed)

Preheat oven to 350° F.
PLACE potatoes in blender container.
ADD cold water to cover.
COVER AND PROCESS on high speed only a few seconds, until potatoes are grated.
DRAIN well.
PLACE remaining ingredients in blender container in the order listed.
COVER AND PROCESS until parsley is chopped.
MIX batter thoroughly with well-drained potatoes.
TURN into greased 1-1/2 quart casserole.
BAKE 1 hour or until brown.
SERVE hot.
MAKES: 6 to 8 servings.

BAKED BEANS

2-1/3 cups great northern beans
water
1/2 pound salt pork, cut in 1-inch pieces
1 cup bean liquid, brought to boiling point
1/4 cup catsup or chili sauce
1/4 cup molasses
4 medium stalks celery, cut up
1 medium-sized onion
2 tablespoons brown sugar
1 teaspoon dry mustard
1/8 teaspoon pepper
1/8 teaspoon ginger
1/2 teaspoon Ac'cent

Preheat oven to 325° F.
SOAK beans in 1-1/2 quarts water overnight.
POUR into large pan.
COOK over low heat about 2-1/2 to 3 hours or until bean skins split.
DRAIN water from beans but *do not discard it.*
PLACE beans in 2-quart casserole with cut up salt pork.
PLACE remaining ingredients in blender container.
COVER AND PROCESS until celery and onions are coarsely chopped.
POUR into beans and stir until thoroughly mixed.
BAKE covered 3 to 4 hours or until beans are soft.
BAKE last half hour without cover to brown top nicely. (If beans become dry during baking, add more bean liquid as needed.)
MAKES: 4 to 6 servings.

BAKED RICE FLUFF

2 cups rice
3 eggs, separated
1/4 medium onion, cut up
1/2 cup butter, melted
1 cup sharp Cheddar cheese, cubed
1 cup parsley

Preheat oven to 350° F.
COOK rice according to package directions and set aside in mixing bowl.

PLACE egg yolks in blender container with onion and butter.
COVER AND BEGIN PROCESSING. While blending,
ADD cheese.
PROCESS until smooth.
ADD parsley and process only long enough to chop. If mixture clings to sides of container, use rubber spatula to push mixture down into blades.
POUR over cooked rice and mix thoroughly.
BEAT egg whites with rotary beater until stiff.
FOLD into rice mixture.
BAKE 25 minutes.
SERVE alone or with creamed seafood.
MAKES: 4 servings.

CURRIED RICE RING

1 cup melted butter
1 medium onion, cut up
1/2 green pepper, cut up
1 can (4 ounces) pimiento
1 can (13 ounces) tomato consommé
3/4 cup water
1/4 teaspoon monosodium glutamate
1/8 teaspoon pepper
1 cup raw quick cooking rice

PLACE butter, cut-up onion, green pepper, pimiento, consommé, water and seasoning in blender container.
COVER AND PROCESS until vegetables are coarsely chopped.
POUR into heavy skillet.
STIR in rice.
COVER tightly.
COOK over medium heat 8 to 10 minutes until rice is cooked. Pack firmly into buttered ring mold, then unmold.
POUR Egg-Mushroom* Filling into center of mold.
MAKES: 6 to 8 servings.

*Egg-Mushroom Filling

1/2 pound fresh mushrooms
2 tablespoons butter
2 tablespoons flour
1/4 teaspoon salt
1 cup milk
1/4 cup sharp Cheddar cheese, cubed
1 tablespoon chili sauce
1/2 teaspoon curry powder
5 hard cooked eggs, cut in eighths

CLEAN mushrooms.
SAUTE in butter in skillet until soft.
REMOVE mushrooms to a large mixing bowl.
ADD more butter, if needed, to skillet to make 2 tablespoons.
ADD flour and salt and stir.
ADD milk and cook over low heat, stirring constantly, for about 3 minutes.
POUR sauce into blender container.
ADD cheese, chili sauce and curry powder.
COVER AND PROCESS until smooth.
ADD cut-up eggs to mushrooms in mixing bowl.
POUR blended mixture over eggs and mushrooms.
STIR until well-mixed.
POUR into center of rice ring.

CHEESE RICE

1/2 cup cooked rice
3/4 cup mushrooms, sliced
1 slice buttered bread
1 cup milk
1 egg
1/2 teaspoon salt
1/8 teaspoon paprika
1/2 teaspoon monosodium glutamate
1 cup cubed Cheddar cheese

Preheat oven to 350° F.
PLACE rice and mushrooms in buttered casserole.
BREAK buttered bread into blender container.
COVER AND PROCESS to crumb.
EMPTY crumbs onto waxed paper.
PLACE milk, egg, salt, paprika, monosodium glutamate and cheese in blender container.

COVER AND PROCESS until smooth and creamy.
POUR over rice and mushroom mixture in casserole.
TOP with bread crumbs.
BAKE 35 to 40 minutes
MAKES: 6 servings.

SEA BREEZE SPINACH MOLD

2 envelopes unflavored gelatine
1/4 cup cold water
1 can (10-1/2 ounces) condensed beef broth, divided
1/4 teaspoon salt
2 tablespoons lemon juice
1 cup salad dressing
1 medium onion, quartered
1 package (10 ounces) frozen chopped spinach, thawed
4 hard-cooked eggs, quartered
1/2 pound bacon, crisply cooked and crumbled
Pimiento strips for garnish

SPRINKLE gelatine over cold water and 1/4 cup beef broth in blender container. Allow to stand while assembling remaining ingredients.
HEAT remaining beef broth to boiling.
ADD to blender container and process at proper speed for gelatine (low) until gelatine dissolves. If any gelatine granules cling to the sides of the container, use a rubber spatula to push them into the mixture. When gelatine is dissolved,
ADD salt, lemon juice and salad dressing.
CONTINUE TO PROCESS until well blended.
STOP BLENDER and add onion.
COVER AND PROCESS until onion is chopped.
STOP BLENDER and add spinach and eggs.
COVER AND PROCESS just until eggs are coarsely chopped.
STIR in bacon.
TURN into 6-cup mold.
CHILL until firm.
UNMOLD.
GARNISH with pimiento strips.
MAKES: 8 servings.

BROCCOLI MOLD

2 envelopes unflavored gelatine
1/2 cup cold water
1 cup boiling water
4 chicken bouillon cubes
1 cup salad dressing
1 tablespoon lemon juice
1/2 medium onion, quartered
1 package (10 ounces) frozen chopped broccoli, cooked 2 to 3 minutes and drained
1/4 cup grated Parmesan cheese
Sliced tomatoes

SPRINKLE gelatine over cold water in blender container. Allow to stand while assembling remaining ingredients.
ADD boiling water and bouillon cubes.
COVER AND PROCESS at proper speed for gelatine (low) until gelatine dissolves. If gelatine granules cling to the sides of the container, use a rubber spatula to push them into the mixture. When gelatine is dissolved,
ADD salad dressing and lemon juice.
COVER AND PROCESS until smooth.
ADD onion, broccoli and cheese.
PROCESS just until onion and broccoli are coarsely chopped.
TURN into 4-cup mold.
CHILL until firm.
UNMOLD and serve with sliced tomatoes.
MAKES: 8 servings.

SPINACH IN ORANGE BUTTER SAUCE

2 packages (10 ounces each) frozen chopped spinach
1 egg yolk
1/2 tablespoon lemon juice
Few grains cayenne
1/4 cup melted butter, bubbling hot
1/4 teaspoon grated orange rind
2 tablespoons orange juice

COOK spinach according to package directions.
MEANWHILE PLACE egg yolk, lemon juice, and cayenne in blender container.
COVER AND PROCESS on low.
REMOVE COVER AND ADD slowly, in a thin stream, 1/4 cup melted butter. When all butter has been added,
STOP BLENDER.
STIR in grated orange rind and juice.
DRAIN cooked spinach thoroughly.
ADD orange butter sauce.
MAKES: 6 servings.

SAUCY PINK CAULIFLOWER

2 packages (10 ounces each) frozen cauliflower
1 jar (4 ounces) pimiento, drained
1 cup milk
2 tablespoons butter or margarine
2 tablespoons flour
1/2 teaspoon salt

COOK cauliflower according to package directions.
DRAIN and keep warm.
PLACE pimiento and milk in blender container.
PROCESS until smooth. Melt butter or margerine in 1 quart saucepan over low heat.
STIR in flour and salt.
ADD pimiento mixture.
COOK and stir constantly until thick and bubbly.
POUR sauce over cauliflower so some of white flowerettes show.
MAKES: 6 servings.

NOODLES SUPREME

1 package (8 ounces) noodles, cooked
1 slice fresh bread
1 cup dairy sour cream
1 package (8 ounces) cream cheese
1/2 small onion, cut up
1/2 teaspoon Worcestershire sauce
1/4 teaspoon garlic salt
Dash of Tabasco
1/2 teaspoon salt

Preheat oven to 350° F.
COOK noodles according to package directions.
SET ASIDE.
BREAK bread into blender container and process to fine crumbs.
SET ASIDE.
PLACE sour cream in blender container.
ADD cream cheese, onion and seasonings.
COVER AND PROCESS until smooth.
PLACE noodles in shallow greased baking dish.
STIR in blended mixture.
SPRINKLE crumbs over top.
BAKE 25 minutes.
MAKES: 4 servings.

CUCUMBER MOUSSE

1 large or 2 small cucumbers, peeled and cut in 1-inch pieces
1 envelope unflavored gelatine
1/4 cup cold water
2 tablespoons boiling water
1 tablespoon lemon juice
6 tablespoons mayonnaise
1 teaspoon Worcestershire sauce
1 teaspoon salt
Dash of white pepper
1 cup creamed cottage cheese
Green food coloring, optional

PLACE cucumber in blender container.
COVER AND PROCESS to purée until smooth. Use only 1-1/2 cups of puréed cucumber.

SOFTEN gelatine in cold water in blender container and add hot water.
COVER AND PROCESS at proper speed for gelatine until gelatine dissolves.
ADD cucumber and remaining ingredients.
COVER AND PROCESS on high speed until smooth. (If desired tint the mixture a pale green with a few drops of food coloring.)
POUR into 1-quart mold or into 8 individual molds.
COVER with aluminum foil and freeze.
DEFROST in refrigerator before serving.
MAKES: 8 servings.

Main Dishes

SHRIMP TEMPURA

1/2 cup sifted flour
1/4 teaspoon salt
1/4 teaspoon baking powder
1 egg
1/3 cup milk
1 tablespoon salad oil
1 pound cooked shrimp, canned or frozen
Oil for frying

PLACE all ingredients except shrimp and oil for frying in blender container.
COVER AND PROCESS until smooth.
POUR into a bowl.
HEAT one inch of oil in a large skillet to 375° F.
DIP shrimp in blended batter.
FRY about 2 or 3 minutes to a golden brown.
REMOVE from pan.
DRAIN on absorbent paper.
SET ASIDE in warm place.
SERVE with Sweet-Sour sauce*.
MAKES: 3 to 4 servings.

**Sweet-Sour Sauce.*

1-1/2 teaspoon cornstarch
1-1/2 teaspoons sugar
1-1/2 teaspoons soy sauce
2-1/2 tablespoons vinegar
2-1/2 teaspoons pineapple juice

PLACE all ingredients in blender container.
COVER AND PROCESS until well mixed.
POUR into saucepan.

COOK over low heat, stirring constantly about 2 or 3 minutes.
SERVE with shrimp.

CREAMED OYSTERS

1 pint oysters
3 slices white bread, crusts removed, divided
1 cup hot milk, divided
2 tablespoons butter
1/2 teaspoon salt
1/8 teaspoon paprika
1/2 teaspoon Worcestershire sauce
1 teaspoon sherry
Patty shells or toast

DRAIN oysters.
BREAK one slice bread in blender container.
ADD about 1/4 cup hot milk, butter and seasonings.
COVER AND PROCESS. With blender running,
ADD remaining bread broken into small pieces and remaining milk.
PROCESS until creamy and smooth.
POUR into saucepan and cook over high heat until mixture comes to boil.
LOWER HEAT and add oysters.
COOK over low heat 10 minutes. (Do not allow sauce to boil.)
SERVE in patty shells or on buttered toast.
MAKES: 3 to 4 servings.

NORWEGIAN FISH PUDDING

1 tablespoon flour
1 teaspoon salt
Dash pepper
1/8 teaspoon nutmeg
1 egg
3 tablespoons softened butter
1/4 cup cream
1 pound trout or haddock, fresh or frozen, cut in pieces
Lemon or tartar sauce

Preheat oven to 325° F.
PLACE all ingredients except fish and lemon or tarter sauce in blender container.

COVER AND PROCESS until smooth.
GRADUALLY ADD uncooked fish and process until smooth. If mixture clings to sides of container use rubber spatula to push mixture down into blades.
TURN into a greased loaf pan and bake 1/2 hour, or until center is firm.
SERVE with lemon or tartar sauce.
MAKES: 4 servings.

SHRIMP MOUSSE ELEGANTE

2 egg whites
2 cups heavy cream
Rounded teaspoon salt
1/2 teaspoon white pepper
1/4 teaspoon nutmeg
1 pound shrimp (raw), cleaned and deveined

Preheat oven to 350° F.
COMBINE egg whites, cream and seasonings in mixing bowl.
POUR 1/3 of this mixture into blender container.
ADD 1/3 of shrimp.
COVER AND PROCESS to a smooth paste. If any of the mixture clings to sides of container, use a rubber spatula to aid in processing.
TURN into well-buttered 1-quart mold.
REPEAT process until all ingredients are used.
COVER mold with aluminum foil.
PLACE in pan with 1 inch of water and bake 45 minutes.
LET STAND in mold 5 minutes.

TURN OUT on warm platter and cover with Sauce Elegante.*
MAKES: 4 to 6 servings.

**Sauce Elegante*

1 can (10-1/2 ounces) condensed cream of mushroom soup
1/3 cup dry white Bordeaux wine
1 tablespoon butter
1/2 teaspoon tarragon (optional)
Dash black pepper
2 sprigs parsley
1/4 pound shrimp (cooked), cleaned and deveined

COMBINE all ingredients in blender container.
COVER AND PROCESS only until shrimp are chopped.
POUR into saucepan.
HEAT slowly until hot.
POUR OVER Shrimp Mousse Elegante.
MAKES: about 2-1/4 cups.

CREAMY NOODLE CASSEROLE

1/2 pound noodles, uncooked
1/2 pound ground beef
1/2 teaspoon salt
1 cup creamed cottage cheese
2 tablespoons sour cream
1 package (3 ounces) cream cheese, cut in cubes
1/2 cup tomato sauce
1 green onion, cut in 1-inch pieces
1 piece (1-inch) green pepper

Preheat oven to 325° F.
COOK noodles according to package directions. Drain, rinse and set aside.
BROWN ground beef in skillet and add salt.
PLACE cottage cheese, sour cream, cream cheese and tomato sauce in blender container.

COVER AND PROCESS until smooth.
ADD onion and green pepper.
COVER AND PROCESS only until finely chopped.
LAYER noodles, meat and sauce in baking dish.
BAKE 45 minutes.
MAKES: 4 servings.

GOLDEN CASSEROLE

3 slices bread, cubed
1 pound carrots, cut in 1-inch pieces
2 eggs
2 cups milk
1/2 pound Cheddar cheese, cubed
1 medium onion, quartered
1/4 cup parsley sprigs

Preheat oven to 350° F.
PLACE 1 slice of bread in blender container.
COVER AND PROCESS until crumbed.
EMPTY into greased casserole.
REPEAT PROCESS with 2 remaining slices of bread.
FILL blender container with carrots.
COVER with water.
COVER AND PROCESS as for raw vegetables only until carrots are grated.
DRAIN in colander and place in casserole with bread crumbs.
REPEAT PROCESS until all carrots are grated.
PLACE remaining ingredients in blender container.
COVER AND PROCESS until smooth.
ADD to grated carrots and bread crumbs and mix well.
BAKE about 45 minutes, or until knife inserted comes out clean.
MAKES: 4 to 6 servings.

QUICHE LORRAINE

- 1 9-inch pie crust, unbaked
- 1/2 pound bacon, fried crisp, drained and crumbled
- 6 ounces Swiss cheese, cubed
- 3 eggs
- 1-1/2 cups light cream
- 1/2 teaspoon salt
- 1/8 teaspoon onion salt
- Dash nutmeg
- Dash pepper

Preheat oven to 375° F.
SPRINKLE bacon over bottom of pie crust.
PLACE half cheese in blender container.
COVER AND PROCESS until finely grated.
SPRINKLE over bacon.
REPEAT with rest of cheese.
PLACE remaining ingredients in blender container.
COVER AND PROCESS at low speed until just combined, but not foamy.
POUR mixture into pie shell.
BAKE 35 to 40 minutes or until golden brown and firm.
REMOVE from oven.
LET STAND 5 to 10 minutes before serving.
MAKES: 6 servings.

TOMATO CHEESE SOUFFLE

- 1 can condensed tomato soup
- 1 cup Cheddar cheese, cut in 1-inch pieces
- Dash of pepper
- 4 eggs, separated
- 8 stuffed olives
- Paprika

Preheat oven to 325° F.
HEAT soup to boiling.
PLACE cheese and pepper in blender container.
ADD about 1/4 hot soup.
COVER AND PROCESS a few seconds.
REMOVE feeder cap and gradually add remaining soup. When smooth,

ADD egg yolks.
CONTINUE processing until well mixed. Just before turning off,
ADD olives and process only until chopped.
POUR into large mixing bowl to cool.
BEAT egg whites until stiff but not dry.
FOLD into soup mixture.
TURN into ungreased 1-1/2-quart casserole.
SPRINKLE with paprika.
BAKE 40 minutes.
SERVE at once.
MAKES: 4 servings.

CHICKEN POT LUCK

1 small onion, sliced
1 tablespoon butter
1 cup cooked chicken or turkey pieces
1 can (10 1/2 ounces) condensed cream of chicken soup
1 soup can water
2 sprigs parsley
1 teaspoon fresh tarragon leaves or 1/3 teaspoon dried tarragon
1/2 cup light cream or milk (cold)

COOK onion in butter in skillet until lightly browned.
COMBINE in blender container with remaining ingredients, except cream or milk.
COVER and process until smooth.
CHILL.
ADD cream or milk before serving.
GARNISH with chopped parsley and chives.
MAKES: 4 servings.

CHEESE FONDUE

1 pound Swiss cheese, cubed
2 tablespoons flour
1 clove garlic
2 cups dry white wine
1/8 teaspoon ground nutmeg
1/4 teaspoon salt
Dash pepper
3 tablespoons Kirsch
Italian or French bread broken into bite-sized pieces to be dipped in fondue

PLACE 1 cup Swiss cheese in blender container.
COVER AND PROCESS until coarsely grated.
EMPTY into bowl.
REPEAT as above with remaining cheese.
ADD flour to cheese and toss lightly.
RUB skillet with garlic.
ADD wine to skillet.
COOK over low heat until wine starts to boil.
SLOWLY ADD cheese, stirring constantly, until mixture is smooth. Keep temperature low.
ADD nutmeg, salt, pepper and Kirsch.
HEAT through.
SERVE from skillet or chafing dish.
MAKES: 4 cups.

CHEESE BLINTZES

2 eggs
1/2 teaspoon salt
1 cup water
1 cup sifted flour
Butter or margarine
3/4 pound cottage cheese, divided
2 tablespoons butter
2 tablespoons coffee cream
1/8 teaspoon salt

PLACE 1 egg, 1/2 teaspoon salt, water and flour in blender container.
COVER AND PROCESS until smooth.
POUR 2 tablespoons batter onto a hot griddle and fry on one side only, using low heat.

REMOVE each pancake onto a clean cloth, uncooked side up.
COOL.
STIR 1/2 pound cottage cheese and the remaining egg and butter together.
SPREAD a little on each pancake and roll.
SAUTE in hot butter.
PLACE coffee cream, remaining cottage cheese and salt in blender container.
COVER AND PROCESS until perfectly smooth.
SPOON onto hot blintzes.
SERVE immediately.
MAKES: 4 servings.

TAHITIAN PORK CHOPS

8 pork chops
3/4 cup sherry or other white wine
1/4 cup soy sauce
1/4 cup salad oil
1 clove garlic
3/4 teaspoon ginger
1/4 teaspoon oregano
1 tablespoon maple syrup

Preheat oven to 350° F.
BROWN pork chops in skillet.
PLACE in baking dish.
PLACE all other ingredients in blender container.
COVER AND PROCESS until smooth.
POUR over chops.
COVER.
BAKE 1 to 1-1/2 hours or until tender.
TURN chops once during baking time to give both sides added browning.
MAKES: 8 servings.

FRENCH HAM AND CHEESE PUFF

1 pound cooked ham, cubed
1/2 pound Swiss cheese, cubed
1/2 cup mayonnaise
1 teaspoon prepared mustard
Dash Worcestershire sauce
Dash onion salt
12 slices French bread
6 eggs
2-1/2 cups milk

Preheat oven to 325° F.
PLACE half of ham in blender container.
COVER AND PROCESS until finely chopped.
EMPTY into bowl.
REPEAT with remaining ham.
PLACE half of Swiss cheese in blender container.
COVER AND PROCESS until finely grated.
EMPTY into bowl containing ham.
REPEAT with remaining cheese.
MIX ham and cheese lightly with mayonnaise, mustard, Worcestershire sauce and onion salt.
SPREAD mixture on six slices of French bread.
TOP with remaining bread to make six sandwiches.
PLACE eggs and milk in blender container.
COVER AND PROCESS until combined.
POUR mixture over sandwiches.
COVER AND REFRIGERATE at least 4 to 6 hours or overnight.
BAKE 30 to 40 minutes or until custard is set.
SERVE by cutting between sandwiches and lifting sandwiches out of baking dish with wide spatula.
MAKES: 6 sandwiches.

CHEESY SCRAMBLED EGGS

6 eggs
1/3 cup light cream
1/2 teaspoon salt
Dash pepper
4 ounces Cheddar cheese, cubed
Butter or shortening

PLACE first five ingredients in blender container.

COVER AND PROCESS just until cheese is finely grated.
MELT butter in skillet over low heat.
POUR in egg mixture. As mixture begins to thicken,
LIFT edges with spatula to let uncooked part go to the bottom.
COOK until eggs are thick and creamy, but still glossy and moist.
SERVE immediately.
MAKES: 4 servings.

HAMBURGER HASH

2 tablespoons shortening
1 pound ground chuck
2 to 3 medium potatoes, peeled and quartered
1 small onion, halved
1/2 green pepper, cubed
1/3 cup light cream
1/2 teaspoon salt
1/8 teaspoon pepper
Dash garlic salt
1/4 cup catsup

MELT shortening in skillet over medium heat.
ADD ground chuck and brown lightly.
MEANWHILE PLACE potatoes, onion and green pepper in blender container.
FILL container to within one to two inches of the top with water.
COVER AND PROCESS until vegetables are coarsely grated.
DRAIN in colander.
ADD drained vegetables, cream and seasonings to ground chuck.
MIX.
PACK firmly in skillet.
COVER AND COOK over medium-low heat 20 minutes or until potatoes are tender.
SPREAD catsup over top of hash.
PLACE under broiler to brown.
SERVE immediately.
MAKES: 6 servings.

HE-MAN CORNED BEEF SANDWICH

1/2 head cabbage
1/2 cup vinegar
1 teaspoon caraway seed
1 teaspoon salt
1/8 teaspoon pepper
3/4 cup water
3/4 cup sour cream
2 teaspoons prepared mustard
1/8 teaspoon Worcestershire sauce
1/8 teaspoon garlic salt
1/4 pound hot sliced corned beef
8 large slices dark rye bread
Dill pickle for garnish

QUARTER cabbage.
CUT quarters in half crosswise.
PLACE half of cabbage in blender container.
FILL container to within one to two inches of top with water.
COVER AND PROCESS until cabbage is coarsely chopped.
DRAIN in colander.
REPEAT with remaining cabbage.
COMBINE cabbage, vinegar, caraway seed, salt and pepper with 3/4 cup water.
BRING quickly to a boil.
REDUCE heat and simmer covered 5 minutes.
STIR occasionally.
DRAIN.
MEANWHILE PLACE sour cream, mustard and seasonings in blender container.
COVER AND PROCESS until smooth.
DISTRIBUTE corned beef evenly over four slices of bread.
TOP each with slaw, sauce, then another slice of bread.
SERVE hot with dill pickles.
MAKES: 4 sandwiches.

HEARTY WELSH RABBIT

2-1/2 cups milk
1/4 cup butter, cubed
1/4 cup flour
1/2 teaspoon salt
1/4 teaspoon onion salt
1 teaspoon dry mustard
1-1/2 teaspoons Worcestershire sauce
Dash pepper
8 ounces Cheddar cheese, cubed
Toast or Holland Rusk

PLACE all ingredients except Cheddar cheese and toast in blender container.
COVER AND PROCESS until blended. With blender continuing to run,
REMOVE feeder cap.
SLOWLY ADD cubed cheese.
COVER AND PROCESS until smooth.
POUR mixture into saucepan.
COOK over moderate heat, stirring constantly until thick.
SERVE hot over toast or Holland Rusk.
MAKES: 6 servings.

INDIVIDUAL HAM LOAVES

2 eggs
1/2 cup mayonnaise
2 teaspoons prepared mustard
1/2 teaspoon salt
Dash Worcestershire sauce
4 cups (1-1/4 pounds) cooked ham, diced
2 slices bread, quartered
6 canned pineapple slices, drained
Brown sugar

Preheat oven to 375° F. Lightly grease 9x9x2-inch baking dish.
PLACE eggs, mayonnaise, mustard, salt and Worcestershire sauce in blender container.
COVER AND PROCESS until smooth. With blender continuing to run,
REMOVE feeder cap from lid.
SLOWLY ADD diced ham and bread.

COVER AND PROCESS until coarsely chopped.
STOP blender and scrape down sides of container with rubber spatula, if necessary.
SHAPE into six individual loaves.
ARRANGE pineapple slices in baking dish.
SPRINKLE with brown sugar.
PLACE ham loaf on each pineapple slice.
BAKE 40-45 minutes or until brown.
MAKES: 6 servings.

MACARONI AND CHEESE

1 pound macaroni, cooked and drained
1 can cream of mushroom soup
1 soup can milk
2 tablespoons prepared mustard
1/8 teaspoon Worcestershire sauce
1/2 cup mayonnaise
2 teaspoons salt
1/2 teaspoon pepper
1 medium onion, cut in quarters
1 pound Cheddar cheese, cubed
Cracker crumbs (optional)
2 tablespoons butter

Preheat oven to 375° F.
PLACE macaroni in greased 2-1/2-quart casserole.
PLACE next eight ingredients in blender container.
COVER AND PROCESS until mixture is smooth and onion is chopped. With blender continuing to run,
REMOVE feeder cap.
SLOWLY ADD cheese.
COVER AND PROCESS until smooth.
STOP BLENDER and scrape down sides of container with rubber spatula, if necessary.
POUR blender mixture over macaroni.
MIX lightly to combine.
SPRINKLE cracker crumbs over top.
DOT with butter.
BAKE 30 to 40 minutes
MAKES: 4 to 6 servings.

MEAT LOAF

2 eggs
1 cup canned tomatoes
1/4 cup catsup
1/2 teaspoon horseradish
1/4 teaspoon Worcestershire sauce
1-1/2 teaspoons salt
1/8 teaspoon pepper
6 slices bread, quartered
1/2 medium green pepper, cut in 2-inch pieces
1 stalk celery, cut in 2-inch pieces
1 medium onion, quartered
1 pound ground chuck

Preheat oven to 350° F. Grease lightly a 9x5x3-inch loaf pan.
PLACE first seven ingredients in blender container.
COVER AND PROCESS until blended. With blender continuing to run,
REMOVE feeder cap.
SLOWLY add quartered bread slices.
COVER AND PROCESS until mixture is smooth.
SLOWLY ADD green pepper, celery and onion.
COVER AND PROCESS until vegetables are finely chopped.
PLACE ground chuck in mixing bowl.
ADD blender mixture.
MIX lightly to combine.
PAT lightly into prepared loaf pan.
BAKE 1 hour or until done.
MAKES: 6 servings.

MOLDED COTTAGE CHEESE, CABBAGE SALAD

1 package (3 ounces) lime flavored gelatin
1 cup hot water
1/4 cup cold water
1-1/2 teaspoons vinegar
1/4 cup salad dressing
1/4 teaspoon salt
1 cup chopped cabbage
1 cup small-curd cottage cheese
1 teaspoon celery seed

PLACE gelatin and hot water in blender container.

COVER AND PROCESS at proper speed for gelatin (low) until gelatin dissolves. With blender continuing to run,
REMOVE feeder cap and slowly add next four ingredients.
COVER AND PROCESS until smooth.
POUR into bowl and chill until syrupy.
ADD cabbage, cottage cheese and celery seed to gelatin mixture.
MIX lightly to combine.
TURN into 1-1/2 quart mold.
CHILL until firm.
MAKES: 6 to 8 servings.

HAM AND CHEESE MACARONI SALAD

3 ounces macaroni, cooked, drained and cooled
1 can (12 ounces) ham, cubed
1 cup Cheddar cheese, cubed
1/2 cup mayonnaise
1/4 cup light cream
1 tablespoon prepared mustard
1/2 teaspoon Worcestershire sauce
3 to 4 green onions and tops, cut in 2-inch pieces
1/4 teaspoon salt
Dash pepper
2 to 3 sweet pickles, plus 2 tablespoons pickle juice
1 2-inch slice pimiento
1/2 medium green pepper, cut in 2-inch pieces
1 large stalk celery, cut in 2-inch pieces

TOSS macaroni, ham and cheese lightly in a large bowl.
PLACE remaining ingredients in blender container.
COVER AND PROCESS until vegetables are chopped.
STOP BLENDER and scrape down sides of container with rubber spatula, if necessary.
ADD to mixture in bowl and fold until combined.
CHILL.
MAKES: 4 servings.

TOMATO TUNA MOLD

1 package (3 ounces) seasoned tomato-flavored gelatin
1/2 cup hot water
1 can (8 ounces) tomato sauce
1 tablespoon lemon juice
1 cup mayonnaise
1 package (8 ounces) softened cream cheese, cubed
2 medium stalks celery, cut in 2-inch pieces
1/2 medium onion, quartered
1/2 medium green pepper, cut in 2-inch pieces
1 can (9-1/4 ounces) tuna, drained and flaked

PLACE gelatin and hot water in blender container.
COVER AND PROCESS at proper speed for gelatin (low) until gelatin dissolves.
STOP BLENDER.
ADD tomato sauce, lemon juice, mayonnaise and cream cheese.
COVER AND PROCESS until smooth. With blender continuing to run,
REMOVE feeder cap and slowly add celery, onion and green pepper.
COVER AND PROCESS until vegetables are coarsely chopped.
TURN in 5-1/2-cup mold.
CHILL until partially set.
FOLD in tuna.
CHILL until firm.
MAKES: 4 to 6 servings.

LOBSTER OR CRABMEAT MOUSSE

- 1 envelope unflavored gelatine
- 1/4 cup cold water
- 1 pound cooked or canned lobster pieces or crabmeat
- 1 can (10-1/2 ounces) condensed cream of mushroom soup
- 1/3 cup whipping cream
- 1/2 cup consommé
- 2-4 drops Tabasco
- 2 teaspoons lemon juice
- Dash nutmeg
- Hard-cooked egg slices, truffles, red pimiento for garnish

SOFTEN gelatine in cold water.
PLACE 1/3 of lobster, mushroom soup and cream in blender container.
COVER AND PROCESS until a fine paste.
EMPTY into bowl.
REPEAT process until all lobster, mushroom soup and cream is used.
COMBINE consommé with softened gelatine.
COOK, stirring constantly, over low heat, until gelatine dissolves. Add to lobster mixture with seasonings.
TURN into 1-quart mold which has been moistened with consommé.
REFRIGERATE 4 to 6 hours.
UNMOLD and decorate with hard-cooked egg slices, truffles and red pimientos.
MAKES: 4 servings.

TAPER-OFF CHICKEN SALAD

1 envelope unflavored gelatine
1/4 cup cold water
3/4 cup boiling water
1 can (10-1/2 ounces) condensed cream of mushroom soup
1 tablespoon lemon juice
2 tablespoons pimiento, diced
1/4 teaspoon salt
1/8 teaspoon pepper
2 cups cooked chicken in chunks
1/2 cup celery pieces
1/4 green pepper, cut in pieces
1 slice onion

SPRINKLE gelatine over cold water in blender container.
ADD boiling water.
COVER AND PROCESS at proper speed for gelatine (low) until gelatine dissolves.
ADD undiluted mushroom soup, lemon juice, salt and pepper.
COVER AND PROCESS at high speed until smooth.
ADD chicken, celery, green pepper and onion.
COVER AND PROCESS until chopped.
STIR in pimiento.
TURN into 4-cup mold.
CHILL until firm.
UNMOLD and serve with salad greens and tomato wedges.
MAKES: 4 servings, 180 calories each.

CREAMY TUNA SALAD

1 envelope unflavored gelatine
1/4 cup cold water
1-1/4 cups boiling water
2 vegetable bouillon cubes
1 teaspoon lemon juice
1/3 cup mayonnaise
1/4 small onion
1 stalk celery, cut into about 1-inch pieces
3 sprigs parsley
3 medium stuffed olives
1 can (6-1/2 or 7 ounces) tuna, drained

SPRINKLE gelatine over cold water in blender container. Allow to stand while assembling remaining ingredients.
ADD boiling water.
COVER AND PROCESS at proper speed for gelatine (low) until gelatine dissolves. If gelatine granules cling to container, use a rubber spatula to push them into the mixture. When gelatine is dissolved,
ADD boullion cubes with remaining ingredients.
COVER AND PROCESS until ingredients are coarsely chopped.
TURN into 1-quart mold.
CHILL until firm.
MAKES: 4 servings.

HAM AND EGG MOLD

1 envelope unflavored gelatine
1/4 cup cold water
1/2 cup boiling water
1/2 cup mayonnaise
3/4 teaspoon salt
1 tablespoon prepared mustard
1/4 green pepper, cut in pieces
1 cup celery pieces
2 whole pimientos
4 hard-cooked eggs, quartered
1 can (4-1/2 ounces) deviled ham

SPRINKLE gelatine over cold water in blender container. Allow to stand while assembling other ingredients.

ADD boiling water.
COVER AND PROCESS at proper speed for gelatine (low) until gelatine dissolves. If gelatine granules cling to container, use a rubber spatula to push them into the mixture.
ADD mayonaise, salt and mustard.
PROCESS until smooth.
STOP BLENDER AND ADD remaining ingredients.
COVER AND PROCESS until chopped.
TURN into 4-cup mold, bowl or 6 to 8 individual molds.
CHILL until firm, about 3 hours for single mold or bowl or 2 hours for individual molds.
MAKES: 6 to 8 servings.

SALMON SALAD MOLD

- 1/3 cup lemon juice
- 2/3 cup water
- 2 envelopes unflavored gelatine
- 1 can (1 pound) salmon
- 1 cup finely chopped cucumber
- 1/2 cup finely chopped green pepper
- 1 jar (4 ounces) pimiento, drained and chopped
- 1 tablespoon finely chopped onion
- 2 teaspoons Worcestershire sauce
- 1/2 teaspoon salt
- 1 cup mayonnaise
- 1 tall can (1-2/3 cups) evaporated milk

COMBINE lemon juice and water in top of double boiler.
SPRINKLE gelatine over top.
SOFTEN 5 minutes.
PLACE over boiling water and stir until gelatine dissolves.
POUR into a medium-size mixing bowl to cool.
REMOVE skin and bones from salmon and discard.
FLAKE salmon in the salmon liquid. When gelatine is cool,
ADD salmon, cucumber, green pepper, pimiento, onion, Worcestershire and salt.

MIX thoroughly.
STIR in mayonnaise, then evaporated milk.
TURN into a well-oiled 2-quart mold.
CHILL until set, about 3 hours.
SERVE with Caper Salad Dressing.*
MAKES: 6 to 8 servings.

**Caper Salad Dressing*

1/2 cup evaporated milk
1/2 cup salad oil
3 tablespoons cider vinegar
1 teaspoon salt
1 tablespoon capers

PLACE all ingredients except capers in blender container.
COVER AND PROCESS a few seconds until smooth and thickened.
STIR in capers.
CHILL.
MAKES: approximately 1 cup.

GOOD CATCH TUNA

2 cans (6-1/2 or 7 ounces each) tuna, drained and flaked
1/2 cup cold tomato juice
2 envelopes unflavored gelatine
1-1/2 cups boiling tomato juice
1 cup mayonnaise
1/2 lemon, peeled and seeded
1 teaspoon dry mustard
1 teaspoon Worcestershire sauce
1/2 teaspoon salt
1/4 teaspoon Tabasco
1 cup celery pieces

PUT tuna into mixing bowl and set aside.
PLACE cold tomato juice and gelatine in blender container.
COVER AND PROCESS at proper speed for gelatine (low) until gelatine is softened.
REMOVE feeder cap and add boiling tomato juice.

CONTINUE TO PROCESS until gelatine dissolves. If gelatine granules cling to container, use a rubber spatula to push them into the mixture. When gelatine is dissolved,
TURN control to highest speed.
ADD mayonnaise, lemon and seasonings.
CONTINUE TO PROCESS until smooth.
STOP BLENDER and add celery.
COVER AND PROCESS until celery is chopped.
ADD to tuna and mix well.
TURN into 5-cup mold or bowl and chill until firm, about 3 hours.
MAKES: 4 servings.

Sauces

WHITE WINE SAUCE VERONIQUE

1/2 cup fish broth
3 tablespoons flour
3/4 teaspoon salt
1/4 teaspoon nutmeg
1/4 teaspoon white pepper
4 tablespoons butter, soft
1 cup milk
1/2 cup dry white Bordeaux wine
2 egg yolks

PLACE all ingredients except wine and egg yolks in blender container.
COVER AND PROCESS until well blended.
EMPTY into saucepan.
SIMMER over low heat, stirring constantly until thickened. Just before serving,
STIR in wine and egg yolk (DO NOT BOIL).
CORRECT seasoning to taste.
MAKES: 2 cups.

SAUCE BERCY

4 shallots or small white onions, cooked
1/4 cup dry white wine
1 can (10-1/2 ounces) condensed cream of celery soup
Dash black pepper
Dash nutmeg
Dash Tabasco
Few drops of lemon juice
2 to 4 tablespoons butter
6 fresh cooked shrimps, cleaned
Sautéed mushrooms or truffles

CUT shallots or onions in pieces.
COMBINE with wine, soup, milk and seasonings in blender container.

COVER and blend until smooth.
POUR into saucepan.
ADD butter.
COOK over low heat until butter is melted and sauce is hot.
GARNISH with shrimp, whole or diced.
ADD sautéed sliced mushrooms or truffles, if desired.
MAKES: about 2 cups.

TOMATO MUSTARD SAUCE

2 tablespoons butter
1 piece celery
2 green onions
2 tablespoons flour
1 teaspoon salt
1/8 teaspoon pepper
1-3/4 cup tomatoes
2 tablespoons prepared yellow mustard
Hamburger patties or sizzling frankfurters

PLACE all ingredients in blender container.
COVER AND PROCESS until vegetables are finely chopped.
POUR mixture into saucepan and simmer over low heat about 5 minutes. To serve:
SPOON desired amount on hamburger patties or spread generously on sizzling franks.
MAKES: 2 cups.

BARBECUE ZING

1/4 cup molasses
1/4 cup prepared yellow mustard
1/4 cup vinegar
2 tablespoons Worcestershire sauce
1 teaspoon tabasco sauce
1/8 teaspoon thyme
1/8 teaspoon oregano
1/4 cup tomato catsup
Hamburgers or frankfurters

PLACE all ingredients in blender container.
COVER AND PROCESS until smooth.
BRUSH on hamburgers or franks while grilling indoors or outdoors.
MAKES: 1 cup.

CREAMY SHRIMP SAUCE

1 cup mayonnaise
1/2 cup sour cream
1 teaspoon dry mustard
1 teaspoon paprika
1 teaspoon lemon juice
1/2 clove garlic
2 sweet pickles, quartered
2 green onions and tops, cut in 2-inch pieces
1 sprig parsley

PLACE all ingredients in blender container.
COVER AND PROCESS to mix until smooth.
REFRIGERATE until serving.
MAKES: 1-1/2 cups.

HONEY GLAZE

1/4 cup soya sauce
1/4 cup honey
1/4 cup lemon juice
1/2 teaspoon celery salt
1/4 cup wine vinegar
1/2 teaspoon dry mustard
1/2 teaspoon ginger

PLACE all ingredients in blender container.
COVER AND PROCESS on low speed until combined.
MAKES: 1 cup.

NIPPY CRANBERRY SAUCE

1 can (1 pound) jellied cranberry sauce
2 tablespoons honey
1 tablespoon horseradish
1 tablespoon salad oil
1 teaspoon prepared mustard
2 teaspoons Worcestershire sauce

PLACE all ingredients in blender container.
COVER AND PROCESS until combined.
REFRIGERATE until serving.
MAKES: 2 cups.

SHRIMP SAUCE

1 cup chili sauce
1/4 cup lemon juice
2 teaspoons horseradish
1/4 medium onion
2 teaspoons Worcestershire sauce
1/4 teaspoon garlic salt
4 drops Tabasco

PLACE all ingredients in blender container.
COVER AND PROCESS until onion is chopped and ingredients are combined.
REFRIGERATE until serving.
MAKES: 1-1/2 cups.

TARTARE SAUCE

1 cup mayonnaise
1 small dill pickle, quartered
Dash Tabasco
1 slice onion
2 sprigs parsley

PLACE all ingredients in blender container.
COVER AND PROCESS until pickle, onion, and parsley are finely chopped and ingredients are combined.
REFRIGERATE until serving.
MAKES: 1 cup.

FISH SAUCE

3 eggs, hard-cooked
6 anchovy fillets
1 medium-sized lemon, peeled, seeded and quartered
Dash of pepper
1/4 teaspoon salt

SEPARATE yolks from egg whites.
SET WHITES aside to use for garnish.
PLACE yolks, anchovies, lemon, pepper and salt in blender container.

COVER AND PROCESS at high speed until smooth.
BRUSH on fish while baking, broiling or barbecuing.
MAKES: 1 cup.

QUICK BARBECUE SAUCE

1 cup catsup
1-1/2 cups water
1 tablespoon flour
3 tablespoons tarragon vinegar
1/4 teaspoon oregano
1/4 teaspoon marjoram
1/8 teaspoon thyme
Dash of garlic salt
1 tablespoon Worcestershire sauce

PLACE all ingredients in blender container.
COVER AND PROCESS at low speed until smooth.
SPREAD on meat while broiling or barbecuing.
MAKES: 2-1/2 cups.

INDIAN CURRY SAUCE

1 cup mayonnaise
1/2 cup catsup
2 anchovies
1/8 green pepper, cut in pieces
2 green onions, cut in 1-inch pieces
4 parsley leaves
1 tablespoon curry powder
1/8 teaspoon cayenne pepper

PLACE all ingredients in blender container.
COVER AND PROCESS at high speed until smooth.
CHILL AND SERVE with lamb, fowl, or fish.
MAKES: 1-1/2 cups.

BLUE CHEESE BASTING SAUCE

1 cup salad oil
1 cup lemon juice
1/2 cup blue cheese
2 tablespoons Worcestershire sauce
1 teaspoon salt
1/4 teaspoon pepper

PLACE all ingredients in blender container.
COVER AND PROCESS until smooth. Excellent sauce for turkey or chicken.
MAKES: 2 cups.

LEMON PARSLEY SAUCE

1/2 cup parsley sprigs
1 medium sized onion, quartered
1/2 teaspoon salt
1 medium-sized lemon, peeled, seeded and quartered

PLACE all ingredients in blender container.
COVER AND PROCESS until smooth.
BRUSH on fish while baking, broiling or barbecuing.
MAKES: 1/2 cup.

MUSTARD SAUCE

1/2 cup cider vinegar
1 egg
2 tablespoons prepared mustard
1 tablespoon soft butter
1 tablespoon sugar
1 tablespoon paprika

PLACE all ingredients in blender container.
COVER AND PROCESS at low speed until smooth.
POUR into saucepan.
COOK over low heat, stirring constantly, until thickened.

SERVE over baked ham or as a dip for shrimp.
MAKES: 3/4 cup.

WINE-BEEF MARINADE

1 cup dry red wine
1/2 cup vinegar
1 cup salad oil
2 onions, quartered
2 cloves garlic
1-1/2 tablespoons salt
1 teaspoon pepper
Dash cayenne pepper
Dash thyme
Dash oregano
4-1/2 pounds chuck pot roast

PLACE all ingredients except pot roast in blender container.
COVER AND PROCESS until smooth.
PLACE pot roast in deep baking dish.
POUR wine marinade over.
COVER well and allow to remain overnight, turning once to be sure both sides are well marinated.
BROIL or barbecue to desired degree of doneness, brushing with sauce which remains.
MAKES: 2-1/2 cups.

DILL SAUCE

1 medium-sized dill pickle, cut in 1-inch pieces
Salt and pepper to taste
1/2 cup sour cream
1 tablespoon prepared mustard

PLACE all ingredients in blender container.
COVER AND PROCESS until smooth.
SERVE with hamburger, ham or pork roast.
MAKES: 1/2 cup.

SWEET-SOUR BASTING SAUCE

1 can (6 ounces) pineapple juice concentrate
2 tablespoons salad oil
1/2 cup wine vinegar
1/3 cup brown sugar
1/8 green pepper
1 slice pimiento
1 teaspoon soy sauce
1/2 clove garlic
1 teaspoon salt
Pineapple chunks and pepper strips for garnish

PLACE all ingredients except garnishes in blender container.
COVER AND PROCESS until smooth.
BRUSH on pork or chicken while it broils, roasts or barbecues.
ADD a few pineapple chunks and green pepper strips for garnish.
MAKES: 1 cup.

TOMATO MUSTARD SAUCE

1-3/4 cups tomatoes, with liquid
1 stalk celery, cut in 1-inch pieces
2 tablespoons prepared mustard
2 tablespoons soft butter
1/8 teaspoon pepper
2 green onions, cut in 1-inch pieces
2 tablespoons flour
1 teaspoon salt

PLACE all ingredients in blender container.
COVER AND PROCESS until vegetables are finely chopped.
POUR into saucepan.
SIMMER about 5 minutes.
SPOON desired amount on each hamburger patty or spread generously on sizzling franks.
MAKES: 2 cups.

WESTERN BAR-B-QUE SAUCE

1 bottle (14 ounces) catsup
1/2 cup undiluted condensed consommé
1/4 cup wine vinegar
1/3 cup salad oil
2 tablespoons soy sauce
1 tablespoon brown sugar
1/8 teaspoon garlic powder
1/2 teaspoon salt

PLACE all ingredients in blender container.
COVER AND PROCESS at low speed until well blended.
HEAT sauce on grill, then use to baste chicken, steak or chops.
MAKES: 2-1/2 cups.

Dressings

SAVORY SALAD DRESSING

- 1 can (1 pound) sliced carrots
- 2 tablespoons white vinegar
- 1 tablespoon lemon juice
- 1 teaspoon instant minced onion
- 1/4 teaspoon garlic salt
- 1/8 teaspoon celery salt
- 1/4 teaspoon Worcestersire sauce
- 1/8 teaspoon Tabasco sauce
- 1/2 cup instant nonfat dry milk (dry form)

DRAIN carrots.
RESERVE liquid.
PLACE carrots, vinegar, lemon juice, onions, garlic salt, celery salt, Worcestershire and Tabasco sauces in blender container.
ADD 2 tablespoons reserved carrot liquid.
COVER AND PROCESS until well blended.
ADD nonfat dry milk.
COVER AND CONTINUE TO PROCESS until very smooth.
MAKES: 1-2/3 cups.
Note: Dressing may be stored in covered container in refrigerator for 5 days.

CREAMY TOMATO SALAD DRESSING

- 1 teaspoon instant minced onion
- 2 teaspoons hot water
- 1 can (8 ounces) tomato sauce
- 2-3 tablespoons lemon juice
- 2 tablespoons finely chopped green pepper
- 1/2 teaspoon garlic salt
- 1/2 teaspoon Worcestershire sauce
- 1/2 teaspoon dry mustard
- 1/2 cup instant nonfat dry milk (dry form)

SOAK instant onion in hot water about 5 minutes.
COMBINE tomato sauce, lemon juice, green pepper, garlic salt, Worcestershire sauce and mustard in blender container.
ADD onions.
COVER AND PROCESS until well blended.
ADD nonfat dry milk.
COVER AND CONTINUE TO PROCESS until very smooth.
CHILL in refrigerator in covered container.
MAKES: 1-1/4 cups.
Note: Dressing may be stored in covered container in refrigerator for 5 days.

HORSERADISH-HERB SALAD DRESSING

- 2 teaspoons prepared horseradish
- 1 tablespoon tarragon vinegar
- 1/4 cup lemon juice
- 3/4 cup water
- 1 tablespoon sugar
- 1 teaspoon salt
- 1 teaspoon dry dill weed
- 1 teaspoon paprika
- 2 cups nonfat dry milk (dry form)

COMBINE all ingredients in blender container.
COVER AND PROCESS as for liquids about 30 seconds or until thoroughly blended.
CHILL in refrigerator about 2 hours in covered container. If thinner dressing is desired, add 1 to 2 table-

spoons liquid nonfat dry milk and process to blend thoroughly.
MAKES: 2 cups.

CELERY SEED SALAD DRESSING

1-1/2 cups sugar
1/2 tablespoon salt
1/2 tablespoon celery seed
1/2 tablespoon paprika
1/2 cup catsup
1/2 tablespoon grated onion
1-1/2 cups salad oil
1/2 cup vinegar

PLACE all ingredients together in blender container.
PROCESS approximately 7 minutes to prevent separating. This amount will keep indefinitely in refrigerator.
MAKES: 3/4 quart.

SEASONED GREEN SALAD DRESSING

1 tablespoon Worcestershire sauce
2 tablespoons cider vinegar
1/4 cup lemon juice
3/4 cup water
1/4 cup coarsely chopped parsley
1/2 teaspoon dry mustard
1/4 teaspoon garlic salt
2 teaspoons sugar
1/4 teaspoon pepper
2-1/2 cups nonfat dry milk (dry form)

COMBINE all ingredients in blender container.
COVER AND PROCESS about 30 seconds or until mixture is thoroughly blended.
CHILL in refrigerator about 2 hours in covered container. If thinner dressing is desired, add 1 to 2 tablespoons liquid nonfat dry milk and reprocess to blend thoroughly.
MAKES: 2 cups.
Note: Dressing may be stored in covered container in refrigerator for 7 days. Stir before using.

ONION SAUCE DELICATE

1 can (10-3/4 ounces) condensed cream of vegetable soup
1/4 to 1/3 cup milk
Dash black pepper
3 small white onions, cooked
4 tablespoons butter
1 teaspoon chopped chives or 1 tablespoon Parmesan for garnish

PLACE soup, milk, pepper and onions in blender container.
COVER AND PROCESS until smooth.
POUR into saucepan.
ADD butter.
COOK slowly, over low heat, until butter is melted and sauce is hot.
ADD 1 teaspoon chopped chives or 1 tablespoon grated Parmesan, if desired.
SERVE over cooked broccoli, asparagus, potatoes or cauliflower or as a sauce for cooked fish steaks or fillets.
MAKES: about 1-1/2 cups.

CARDAMOM SALAD DRESSING FOR FRUITS

1/2 cup evaporated milk
1/2 cup salad oil
1/4 cup lemon juice
1/2 teaspoon salt
1 teaspoon sugar
1/4 teaspoon ground cardamom

PLACE all ingredients in blender container.
COVER AND PROCESS a few seconds until smooth and thickened.
CHILL.
SERVE with fruits of your choice: cantaloupe slices, avocado rings, banana chunks, seedless grapes, blueberries, pineapple slices, peach halves, orange and grapefruit sections.
MAKES: 1-1/4 cups.

BLENDER BLUE CHEESE DRESSING

1/2 cup evaporated milk
1/2 cup salad oil
1 teaspoon onion salt
2 ounces (1/3 cup) blue cheese
3 tablespoons cider vinegar

PLACE all ingredients in blender container.
COVER AND PROCESS a few seconds until smooth and thickened.
CHILL, tightly covered, in refrigerator.
SERVE over wedges of lettuce, crisp mixed greens, sliced tomatoes, tomato aspic, or as a dressing on open-face sandwiches of sliced chicken, turkey or ham.
MAKES: about 1-1/2 cups.

ANCHOVY SALAD DRESSING

1 cup evaporated milk
1/2 cup salad oil
1/4 cup wine vinegar
1 teaspoon salt
Dash of garlic powder
1/4 cup parsley pieces
2 cans (2 ounces each) flat fillets of anchovies, drained
1/4 teaspoon pepper

PLACE all ingredients in blender container.
COVER AND PROCESS a few seconds until smooth.
CHILL and serve with Antipasto Salad.
MAKES: about 2 cups.

PIQUANT HERB FRENCH DRESSING

3/4 cup corn oil
1/4 cup cider vinegar
1 tablespoon tarragon vinegar
White of 1 hard-cooked egg
2 teaspoons capers
1/2 teaspoon salt
1/2 teaspoon prepared mustard
Dash pepper
2 small sprigs parsley
1 blade chive

PLACE all ingredients in blender container in order given.
COVER AND PROCESS 30 to 40 seconds until mixture is slightly thickened.
MAKES: about 1 cup.

PIQUANT MAYONNAISE DRESSING

3/4 cup mayonnaise
1 tablespoon tarragon vinegar
White of 1 hard-cooked egg
2 teaspoons capers
1/2 teaspoon prepared mustard
2 small sprigs parsley
1 blade chive

PLACE all ingredients in blender container in order given.
COVER AND PROCESS 30 to 40 seconds until mixture is slightly thickened. If mixture clings to sides of container, stop blender and scrape sides with rubber spatula.
MAKES: 3/4 cup.

ROSY FRENCH DRESSING

1/4 cup vinegar
3/4 cup sugar
1/2 teaspoon dry mustard
1/4 teaspoon salt
1 cup corn oil
1 cup catsup
1/2 teaspoon celery seed
1/2 teaspoon minced onion

PLACE vinegar, sugar, dry mustard and salt in blender container.
COVER AND PROCESS 30 seconds until sugar is almost dissolved.
SLOWLY add corn oil, keeping blender running.
STIR in catsup, celery seed and onion.
COVER AND PROCESS about 30 seconds until dressing is smooth.
MAKES: 2-1/2 cups.

SPICY MAYONNAISE DRESSING

3/4 cup mayonnaise
1 tablespoon cider vinegar
2 tablespoons water
1 tablespoon catsup
1 teaspoon sugar
1/4 teaspoon pepper
2 tablespoons hamburger relish

PLACE all ingredients in blender container.
COVER AND PROCESS about 1 minute until ingredients are well mixed.
CHILL.
MAKES: 1 cup.

SPICY RELISH DRESSING

3/4 cup corn oil
3 tablespoons cider vinegar
2 tablespoons water
2 tablespoons hamburger relish
1 tablespoon catsup
1 teaspoon sugar
1/2 teaspoon salt
1/4 teaspoon pepper

PLACE all ingredients in blender container.
COVER AND PROCESS about 1 minute until ingredients are well mixed.
CHILL.
MAKES: 1-1/4 cups.

GREEN MAYONNAISE

12 spinach leaves
12 watercress leaves
8 sprigs parsley
9 sprigs fresh chervil
9 sprigs fresh tarragon
1 clove garlic, halved
1 cup mayonnaise

BLANCH fresh greens in boiling water 2 minutes.
DRAIN, reserving 2 tablespoons liquid.
RUB inside of blender container with cut side of garlic and discard.
PLACE blanched greens and liquid in blender container and process 30 seconds to purée.
STIR into mayonnaise.
CHILL.
SERVE on chilled fish or vegetable salad.
MAKES: 1-1/3 cups.
Note: 1 teaspoon dried chervil leaves and dried tarragon leaves may be substituted for fresh herbs. Stir into mayonnaise with blanched greens.

THOUSAND ISLAND DRESSING

1-1/2 cups mayonnaise
1/3 cup chili sauce
1/4 onion, halved
2 sweet pickles, quartered
1 slice green pepper
1 teaspoon lemon juice
2 hard-cooked eggs, halved

PLACE all ingredients except eggs in blender container.
COVER AND PROCESS until vegetables are chopped.
STOP BLENDER and scrape sides of container with rubber spatula, if necessary. With blender continuing to run,
REMOVE feeder cap and slowly add eggs.
COVER AND PROCESS only until eggs are coarsely chopped.
REFRIGERATE until serving.
MAKES: 2 cups.

ROQUEFORT DRESSING

1 pint sour cream
1/2 cup mayonnaise
2 tablespoons wine vinegar
1 slice onion
1 small clove garlic, split
1 teaspoon salt
8 ounces Roquefort cheese

PLACE all ingredients except cheese in blender container.
COVER AND PROCESS until smooth. With blender continuing to run,
REMOVE feeder cap and slowly add Roquefort.
COVER AND PROCESS until combined.
REFRIGERATE until serving.
MAKES: 3-1/2 cups.

MAYONNAISE SLAW DRESSING

1 cup mayonnaise
1/4 cup light cream
1/4 cup vinegar
1/4 cup sugar
3/4 teaspoon salt
1/4 teaspoon pepper

PLACE all ingredients in blender container.
COVER AND PROCESS until thoroughly blended.
REFRIGERATE until serving.
MAKES: 1-1/2 cups.

MAYONNAISE

1 egg
1/2 teaspoon dry mustard
1/2 teaspoon salt
1/4 teaspoon paprika
2 tablespoons lemon juice or vinegar
1 cup salad oil, divided

PLACE all ingredients except one-half cup salad oil in blender container.
COVER AND PROCESS until thick and well blended.
STOP BLENDER and scrape down sides of container with rubber spatula, if necessary. With blender continuing to run,
REMOVE feeder cap and slowly add remaining oil.
REFRIGERATE until serving.
MAKES: 1 cup.

CREAMY SLAW DRESSING

1 cup creamed cottage cheese
1/2 cup sour cream
1/4 cup vinegar
1/4 cup sugar
3/4 teaspoon salt
1/4 teaspoon pepper

PLACE all ingredients in blender container.
COVER AND PROCESS until creamy.
REFRIGERATE until serving.
MAKES: 1-1/2 cups.

GREEN GODDESS DRESSING

1 cup mayonnaise
2 tablespoons anchovy paste
1 teaspoon Worcestershire sauce
1 teaspoon lemon juice
1/2 teaspoon dry mustard
1 clove garlic, split
3 green onions and tops, cut in 2-inch pieces
4 to 6 cooked shrimp
1 hard-cooked egg, halved

PLACE all ingredients except onion, shrimp and egg in blender container.
COVER AND PROCESS until smooth. With blender continuing to run,
REMOVE feeder cap and slowly add remaining ingredients.
COVER AND PROCESS until finely chopped.
REFRIGERATE until serving.
MAKES: 1-1/2 cups.

FRUIT SALAD DRESSING

3/4 cup salad oil
1/4 cup lemon juice
1/2 cup wine vinegar
1/4 cup honey
1/4 cup catsup
1 teaspoon horseradish
1/2 teaspoon Worcestershire sauce
1/2 teaspoon salt
1/2 medium onion, quartered

PLACE all ingredients in blender container.
COVER AND PROCESS until smooth.
REFRIGERATE until serving.
MAKES: 2 cups.

FRENCH DRESSING

1/2 cup salad oil
2 tablespoons vinegar
2 tablespoons lemon juice
2 teaspoons sugar
1/2 teaspoon dry mustard
1/2 teaspoon paprika
1/2 teaspoon salt
1/2 teaspoon onion salt
Dash garlic salt
Dash pepper

PLACE all ingredients in blender container.
COVER AND PROCESS until combined.
REFRIGERATE until serving.
MAKES: 3/4 cup.

HONEY SUNSHINE DRESSING

1/2 cup honey
1/4 cup lemon juice
1/4 cup lime juice
1 teaspoon salt
1 teaspoon dry mustard
1 teaspoon paprika
1 teaspoon celery seed
3/4 cup salad oil

PLACE all ingredients except salad oil in blender container.
COVER AND PROCESS until combined.
STOP BLENDER and scrape down sides of container with rubber spatula, if necessary. With blender continuing to run,
REMOVE feeder cap and gradually add salad oil.
COVER AND PROCESS until thick and creamy.
REFRIGERATE until serving.
MAKES: 1-3/4 cups.

AVOCADO DRESSING

1 ripe avocado, peeled and diced
Juice of 1 lemon
Peel of 1 lemon
2 tablespoons honey
1/4 teaspoon salt
1/2 cup heavy cream

PLACE all ingredients except cream in blender container.
COVER AND PROCESS until smooth. With blender continuing to run,
REMOVE feeder cap and slowly add cream.
STOP BLENDER and scrape down sides of container with rubber spatula, if necessary.
COVER AND PROCESS until smooth and fluffy.
REFRIGERATE until serving.
MAKES: 1 cup.

Breads

FRUIT AND NUT BREAD

1-1/4 cups sifted flour
1 teaspoon baking powder
1/2 teaspoon salt
1/2 teaspoon soda
1 cup whole bran
1/2 cup walnuts
2 eggs
1/3 cup shortening
2/3 cup sugar
1/4 cup buttermilk
3 ripe bananas, sliced in 1/2-inch pieces
1 cup dried apricots

Preheat oven to 350° F. Grease 9x5x3-inch loaf pan.
SIFT together flour, baking powder, salt and soda in medium bowl.
ADD whole bran.
PLACE nuts in blender container.
COVER AND PROCESS until coarsely chopped.
ADD to flour mixture.
PLACE eggs, shortening, sugar and milk in blender container.
COVER AND PROCESS until well blended. With blender continuing to run,
REMOVE feeder cap and slowly add bananas.
COVER AND PROCESS until completely liquified.
ADD apricots. Cover and process until apricots are coarsely chopped.
ADD to dry ingredients.
STIR well.
TURN into prepared pan.
BAKE 45 minutes or until cake tester inserted comes out clean.
MAKES: 1 loaf.

OATMEAL NUT BREAD

- 1-1/2 cups sifted flour
- 1/2 teaspoon salt
- 1/2 teaspoon baking powder
- 1 teaspoon baking soda
- 3/4 cup quick-cooling oatmeal
- 1 egg
- 1/2 cup sugar
- 1 cup sour cream
- 1/3 cup dark molasses
- 1/2 cup pitted dates
- 1 cup nuts

Preheat oven to 350° F. Line a greased 8-1/2 x 4-1/2-inch loaf pan with waxed paper, and then grease waxed paper.
SIFT flour, salt, baking powder and baking soda into mixing bowl.
ADD oatmeal.
PLACE egg, sugar, sour cream and molasses in blender container.
COVER AND PROCESS on high speed until smooth and well blended. With blender continuing to run,
REMOVE feeder cap and slowly add dates and nuts.
COVER AND PROCESS until dates are chopped.
EMPTY into dry ingredients and stir well.
FILL prepared pan.
BAKE 45 to 55 minutes or until bread tests done.
MAKES: 1 loaf.

CRANBERRY-NUT BREAD

- 2 cups sifted flour
- 1-1/2 teaspoons baking powder
- 1/2 teaspoon soda
- 1 egg
- 1/4 cup shortening
- 1 teaspoon salt
- 1 1x2-inch piece orange rind
- 1 cup sugar
- 3/4 cup orange juice
- 1/2 cup nuts
- 1 cup cranberries

Preheat oven to 350° F. Grease loaf pan.
SIFT flour, baking powder and baking soda into mixing bowl.

PLACE egg, shortening, salt, orange rind, sugar and orange juice in blender container.
COVER AND PROCESS until rind is grated fine.
ADD nuts and cranberries.
COVER AND PROCESS until chopped.
EMPTY into flour mixture and mix only until blended.
SPOON into prepared pan.
BAKE 50-60 minutes or until cake tester inserted comes out clean.
MAKES: 1 loaf.

CHEESE MUFFINS

2 cups sifted flour
4 teaspoons baking powder
1 tablespoon sugar
1/2 teaspoon salt
1 egg
1 cup milk
3 tablespoons soft butter
1/2 pound sharp Cheddar cheese, cubed

Preheat oven to 350° F. Grease muffin tins well.
SIFT flour, baking powder, sugar and salt into mixing bowl.
PLACE egg, milk, and butter in blender container.
COVER AND PROCESS until well blended. With blender continuing to run,
REMOVE feeder cap and slowly add cheese.
COVER AND PROCESS until cheese is finely chopped.
POUR into dry ingredients and mix only until flour is moistened.
FILL prepared tins 2/3 full.
BAKE 15 to 25 minutes or until muffins test done.
MAKES: 12 muffins.

POPOVERS

1 cup milk
2 eggs
1 cup sifted flour
1/2 teaspoon salt

Preheat oven to 450° F.
PLACE all ingredients in blender container.
COVER AND PROCESS until smooth.
FILL greased muffin tins or custard cups 1/2 full.
BAKE 10 minutes.
LOWER oven heat to 350° F. and bake 35 minutes.
SERVE while hot.
MAKES: 8 popovers.

SNAPPY PICNIC MUFFINS

3 cups sifted flour
1-1/2 teaspoons baking soda
1 egg
1 cup molasses
1/2 cup soft shortening
1/2 cup sugar
1 teaspoon cinnamon
1 teaspoon ginger
1/2 teaspoon salt
1/2 teaspoon cloves
1 cup hot water

Preheat oven to 375° F. Grease muffin tins.
SIFT flour and baking soda together in large mixing bowl. Set aside.
PLACE remaining ingredients except hot water in blender container.
COVER AND PROCESS until smooth.
REMOVE feeder cap and add hot water.
CONTINUE TO PROCESS until well blended.
POUR into flour and mix well.
FILL muffin tins 2/3 full.
BAKE about 20 minutes or until muffins test done.
WRAP in foil and heat on outdoor grill, if desired.
MAKES: 18 muffins.

PANCAKES

- 1 cup milk
- 1 egg
- 2 tablespoons melted shortening
- 1-1/4 cups sifted flour
- 3 teaspoons baking powder
- 1 tablespoon sugar
- 1/2 teaspoon salt

PLACE milk, egg and shortening in blender container.
COVER AND PROCESS just until combined. With blender continuing to run,
REMOVE feeder cap and slowly add dry ingredients.
COVER AND PROCESS only until moistened.
STOP BLENDER and scrape down sides of container, if necessary.
BAKE on lightly greased griddle until golden brown.
TURN only once.
MAKES: 8 large pancakes.

SOUR MILK PANCAKES

- 1 cup sour milk or buttermilk
- 1 egg
- 1 tablespoon sugar
- 1 cup sifted flour
- 1 teaspoon baking soda
- 1/2 teaspoon salt
- 1 tablespoon melted shortening or salad oil

PLACE all ingredients in blender container.
COVER AND PROCESS until well blended.
STOP BLENDER and scrape down sides of container with rubber spatula, if necessary.
BAKE on a lightly greased griddle until golden brown.
TURN only once.
MAKES: 8 to 10 pancakes.

POTATO PANCAKES

2 eggs
1/2 small onion
1 teaspoon salt
1/4 cup flour
1/4 teaspoon baking powder
2 cups cubed raw potato

PLACE all ingredients in blender container in the order listed.
COVER AND PROCESS at low speed.
TURN to high speed and continue processing until potatoes are grated.
STOP BLENDER and scrape down sides of container with rubber spatula, if necessary.
DO NOT OVERBLEND. Pour batter onto a hot well-greased griddle.
BROWN on both sides.
DRAIN on absorbent paper.
MAKES: 8 to 10 pancakes.

DRIED BEEF PANCAKES

2 cups pancake mix
1-3/4 cups milk
1 egg
2 tablespoons shortening
1/2 teaspoon prepared mustard
1 cup dried beef

PLACE pancake mix, milk, egg, shortening and mustard in blender container.
COVER AND PROCESS until smooth.
ADD dried beef.
COVER AND PROCESS on high until finely chopped.
STOP BLENDER and scrape sides of container with rubber spatula, if necessary.
POUR small amounts on lightly greased griddle.
BROWN on one side, turn and brown on other side.
MAKES: 16 to 18 pancakes.

BLUEBERRY PANCAKES

1 cup sifted flour
1/2 teaspoon baking soda
3/4 teaspoon baking powder
1/2 cup fresh, canned or frozen blueberries, drained
1 egg
1 cup buttermilk
1 tablespoon butter, melted
1/2 teaspoon salt

SIFT flour, soda and baking powder into a mixing bowl.
ADD blueberries.
PLACE remaining ingredients in blender container.
COVER AND PROCESS until thoroughly blended.
ADD to dry ingredients.
MIX just enough to dampen the dry ingredients (leave lumpy).
DROP by tablespoonfuls onto a lightly greased griddle.
BAKE until brown.
TURN only once.
MAKES: 8 to 10 pancakes.

APPLE PANCAKES

1 egg
1 tablespoon sugar
1 tablespoon softened butter
1 medium apple, peeled, cored and quartered
1 cup evaporated milk
1 cup packaged pancake mix

PLACE egg, sugar, butter, apple and evaporated milk in blender container.
COVER AND PROCESS a few seconds until apple is chopped.
ADD pancake mix.
COVER AND PROCESS a few seconds longer until blended.
POUR about 1/4 cup at a time onto preheated hot (400°F) electric griddle.

BAKE until bubbles appear on top and underside is browned.
TURN and bake to brown second side.
SERVE hot with Cinnamon cream syrup.*
MAKES: 4 to 5 servings.

**Cinnamon Cream Syrup.*

1 cup light corn syrup
2 cups sugar
1/2 cup water
2 teaspoons cinnamon
1 cup evaporated milk

COMBINE corn syrup, sugar, water and cinnamon in medium size saucepan.
BRING to a full boil over medium heat, stirring constantly.
CONTINUE STIRRING and boiling for an additional 2 minutes.
COOK 5 minutes.
STIR in evaporated milk.
SERVE warm over Apple Pancakes.
MAKES: about 3 cups.

CORN FRITTERS

1 cup sifted flour
1 teaspoon baking powder
3/4 teaspoon salt
1/8 teaspoon paprika
2 eggs, separated
2 cups whole kernel corn, drained, divided
1/4 cup liquid from corn
Fat for frying

Heat fat to 365°.
SIFT dry ingredients together.
PLACE the egg yolks, 1 cup corn and corn liquid in blender container.
COVER AND PROCESS until well blended.
ADD half the dry ingredients and process about 20 seconds.
STOP BLENDER and scrape down sides of container with rubber spatula, if necessary.

ADD remaining dry ingredients.
COVER AND PROCESS until mixed.
ADD remaining corn just before turning off blender.
BEAT egg whites until stiff.
GRADUALLY FOLD in blended mixture.
DROP from tablespoon into hot fat.
FRY until golden brown on all sides.
DRAIN on absorbent paper.
SERVE hot with maple syrup.
MAKES: 12 to 18 fritters.

FRUIT COCKTAIL FRITTERS

1-1/2 cups sifted flour
1-1/2 teaspoons baking powder
1/2 teaspoon salt
1 tablespoon sugar
1/2 cup milk
2 eggs
1 cup well-drained fruit cocktail
Fat for frying

Heat fat to 375° F.
SIFT dry ingredients together.
PLACE milk and eggs in blender container.
COVER AND PROCESS until well mixed.
STOP BLENDER.
ADD flour mixture.
COVER AND PROCESS until dry ingredients are just moistened.
STIR in well-drained fruit.
DROP batter from tablespoon into hot fat.
FRY until golden brown on all sides.
DRAIN.
SERVE while hot as a hot bread, with butter or syrup.
MAKES: about 15 fritters.

APPLE FRITTERS

1-1/2 cups sifted flour
1/4 cup sugar
1/8 teaspoon salt
2 teaspoons baking powder
1/2 cup milk
2 eggs
2 cooking apples, washed, cored and quartered
Fat for frying
Powdered sugar

Heat fat to 370° F.
SIFT flour, sugar, salt and baking powder together into medium bowl.
PLACE milk, eggs and apples in blender container.
COVER AND PROCESS until apples are coarsely chopped.
DO NOT OVERBLEND.
ADD apple mixture to dry ingredients in bowl.
STIR until batter is smooth.
DROP batter by teaspoonfuls into hot fat.
FRY until fritters are golden brown.
DRAIN on absorbent paper.
SPRINKLE with powdered sugar.
MAKES: about 30 fritters.

BATTER FOR WAFFLES

2 eggs
1-1/2 cups milk
1/2 cup melted shortening
1/4 teaspoon salt
2 cups sifted flour
2 teaspoons baking powder
2 teaspoons sugar

PLACE eggs, milk and shortening in blender container.
COVER AND PROCESS on high speed until smooth.
ADD remaining ingredients.
COVER AND PROCESS until almost smooth.
STOP BLENDER and scrape down sides of container with rubber spatula, if necessary.
BAKE according to manufacturer's directions on waffle iron.
MAKES: 3 cups batter.

Cakes, Pies and Cookies

BERRY TORTE

16 graham crackers
1/2 cup sugar
1/4 cup melted butter
2 eggs
1 package (8 ounces) cream cheese, softened, cut in fourths
1 cup sugar
1 package frozen berries (strawberries, raspberries, blueberries)
1 tablespoon lemon juice
1/2 cup sugar
1 tablespoon cornstarch

Preheat oven to 350° F.
BREAK half of graham crackers in blender container.
COVER AND PROCESS to crumb.
EMPTY into a bowl.
REPEAT with remaining crackers. Add 1/2 cup sugar and butter to crumbs in bowl.
MIX lightly until moistened.
PRESS into a 9x9x2-inch pan.
PLACE eggs and softened cream cheese in blender container.
COVER AND PROCESS until smooth.
STOP BLENDER and scrape down sides of container with rubber spatula, if necessary. With blender continuing to run,
REMOVE feeder cap and slowly add 1 cup sugar.
COVER AND PROCESS until well blended.
SPREAD cream cheese mixture over crust.
BAKE 25 to 30 minutes or until firm.
COOL.
MEANWHILE DRAIN JUICE from berries.
MIX berry liquid with lemon juice, 1/2 cup sugar and cornstarch in small saucepan.

COOK over medium heat until mixture is thick and clear.
ADD berries.
SPREAD over cheese mixture.
CHILL before serving.
MAKES: 6 to 8 servings.

APRICOT POUND CAKE

- 1 can (1 pound) apricot halves
- 1 package yellow cake mix (regular size)
- 1 package (3 ounces) lemon-flavored gelatin
- 3/4 cup salad oil
- 4 eggs
- 2 teaspoons lemon extract

Preheat oven to 350° F.
PLACE apricots and juice together in blender container.
PROCESS to purée.
PLACE 1 cup purée mixture in large mixing bowl.
ADD cake mix, gelatin, oil, eggs and extract.
MIX about 5 minutes on medium speed.
TURN into well-greased and floured tube pan.
BAKE 50 minutes or until well browned. Cake will pull away from side of pan. While cake is still warm,
SPOON "Apricot Drizzle"* over entire cake.
COOL before serving.
MAKES: 8 to 12 servings.

**Apricot Drizzle*

- Juice of 1 lemon
- 1/2 stick butter or margarine
- 3 tablespoons apricot purée
- 1-1/2 cups powdered sugar

COMBINE all ingredients in saucepan and heat slowly (BUT DO NOT BOIL) until sugar is dissolved and butter melted. Mixture will be thin.

TWO-EGG CAKE

2 cups sifted cake flour
2-1/2 teaspoons baking powder
1 teaspoon salt
1/2 cup milk
2 eggs
1/2 cup shortening
1-1/4 teaspoons vanilla
1 cup sugar

Preheat oven to 375° F. Grease and wax paper line two 8-inch layer cake pans.
SIFT flour, baking powder and salt together.
PLACE remaining ingredients in blender container. n
COVER AND PROCESS at high speed until smooth.
STOP BLENDER and scrape down sides of container with rubber spatula, if necessary.
ADD dry ingredients.
COVER AND PROCESS about 5 seconds.
INCREASE speed to high and process about 50 seconds or until just mixed.
TURN into prepared pans.
BAKE 25 minutes or until cake tester inserted comes out clean.
COOL on racks.
FROST.
MAKES: 1 cake.

BANANA CAKE

2 cups sifted flour
1 teaspoon baking powder
1 teaspoon baking soda
1/2 teaspoon salt
1-1/4 cups sugar
1/2 cup shortening
1/2 cup buttermilk
1-1/2 cups sliced bananas
2 eggs
1 teaspoon vanilla
1/2 cups nuts

Preheat oven to 350° F. Grease and flour two 8-inch cake pans.

SIFT flour, baking powder, baking soda and salt together in large mixing bowl.
PLACE sugar, shortening, buttermilk, bananas, eggs and vanilla in blender conntainer.
COVER AND PROCESS at high speed until smooth.
STOP BLENDER and scrape down sides of container with rubber spatula, if necessary. With blender continuing to run,
REMOVE feeder cap and slowly add nuts.
COVER AND PROCESS until nuts are coarsely chopped.
POUR mixture over dry ingredients and mix well.
TURN into prepared pans.
BAKE 30 to 40 minutes.
COOL in pan 5 minutes before serving.
MAKES: two 8-inch layers.

COCOA-APPLESAUCE CAKE

2 cups sifted cake flour
2 tablespoons cocoa
1 teaspoon salt
1-1/2 teaspoons baking powder
1/2 teaspoon soda
1 teaspoon cinnamon
1/2 teaspoon cloves
1/2 teaspoon nutmeg
1/2 teaspoon allspice
2 eggs
1/2 cup shortening
1-3/4 cups sugar
3/4 cup raisins
3 medium apples, cored and cubed

Preheat oven to 350° F. Grease and wax paper line 13x9x2-inch pan.
SIFT flour, cocoa, salt, baking powder, soda and spices in medium mixing bowl.
PLACE eggs, shortening, sugar and raisins in blender container.
COVER AND PROCESS at high speed until smooth.
STOP BLENDER and scrape down sides of container with rubber spatula, if necessary. With blender continuing to run,
REMOVE feeder cap and slowly add apples.
COVER AND PROCESS until smooth.

POUR mixture over dry ingredients.
MIX well.
TURN batter into prepared pan.
BAKE 45 minutes or until cake tester inserted comes out clean.
MAKES: 1 cake.

CHRISTMAS BRUNCH CAKE

1 cup pecans
1/4 cup melted butter
1/4 cup white sugar
1/3 cup brown sugar
1 teaspoon cinnamon
14 green maraschino cherries, well drained
2-1/4 cups sifted flour
1 teaspoon baking powder
1 teaspoon baking soda
1/2 teaspoon salt
2 eggs
1/2 cup soft shortening
1 cup sugar
1 teaspoon vanilla extract
1 cup sour cream

Preheat oven to 350° F. Grease a "Turban" or "Baba" mold or similar fluted tube mold very well.
PLACE pecans in blender container.
COVER AND PROCESS to chop.
EMPTY into small bowl and combine with butter, sugars and cinnamon.
PRESS mixture on bottom and sides of prepared mold.
PLACE cherries into blender container.
COVER AND PROCESS as for nuts. Spread on absorbent paper to remove as much moisture as possible.
SIFT flour, baking powder, baking soda and salt together in large mixing bowl.
ADD cherries and mix well to distribute cherries throughout.
PLACE eggs, shortening, sugar and vanilla in blender container.
COVER AND PROCESS at high speed until mixture is smooth.
ADD sour cream and continue to process only until thoroughly blended.
POUR over flour mixture.
STIR well to combine all ingredients.
SPOON into mold, spreading evenly.

BAKE 45 to 55 minutes or until cake tests done.
COOL 5 minutes before removing from pan.
MAKES: 1 cake.

LOW-CALORIE CHEESECAKE

2 envelopes unflavored gelatine
1/2 cup cold skimmed milk
1 cup skimmed milk, heated to boiling
Rind of 1 lemon (use vegetable peeler to remove rind in thin strips
1 lemon, peeled and seeded
1 cup sugar, divided
2 eggs, separated
1/4 teaspoon salt
3 cups (24 ounces) creamed cottage cheese
1 teaspoon vanilla
1/3 cup graham cracker crumbs
1/8 teaspoon each cinnamon and nutmeg

SPRINKLE gelatine over cold milk in blender container. Allow to stand while assembling remaining ingredients.
ADD boiling milk.
COVER AND PROCESS at proper speed for gelatine (low) until gelatine dissolves.
ADD lemon rind, lemon, 3/4 cup sugar, egg yolks and salt.
COVER AND PROCESS at high speed until rind is in very tiny pieces.
ADD cottage cheese and vanilla.
COVER AND CONTINUE PROCESSING at high speed until smooth.
TURN into bowl and chill, stirring occasionally, until mixture mounds slightly when dropped from spoon.
BEAT egg whites until stiff but not dry.
GRADUALLY ADD remaining 1/4 cup sugar and beat until very stiff.
FOLD into gelatine mixture.
COMBINE graham cracker crumbs with spices.
SPRINKLE about half of mixture over bottom of 8-inch spring-form pan.
TURN gelatine mixture into pan.
SPRINKLE remaining crumbs over top.

CHILL until firm.
MAKES: 12 to 16 servings, 165 calories for 1/12 of cake and 125 calories for 1/16 of cake.

SPICE-NUT APPLESAUCE CAKE

1-1/2 cups sifted flour
2 teaspoons baking powder
1/2 teaspoon baking soda
1/2 teaspoon salt
1/2 teaspoon cinnamon
1/2 teaspoon nutmeg
1/2 teaspoon ground cloves
1/2 cup raisins
1 teaspoon ascorbic acid powder
1 tablespoon water
3 medium apples, seeded and cut in eighths
1 egg
1/2 cup soft shortening
1 cup sugar
1/2 cup walnuts

Preheat oven to 350° F. Grease and flour 9x9x2-inch pan.
SIFT dry ingredients together in large mixing bowl.
ADD raisins.
PLACE ascorbic acid powder, water and 4 or 5 pieces of apple in blender container.
COVER AND PROCESS until apples are puréed.
REMOVE feeder cap and gradually add remaining apple pieces.
COVER AND PROCESS until all apples are puréed.
REMOVE from container and measure 1 cup of applesauce.
ADD to flour mixture.
PLACE EGG, shortening and sugar in blender container.
COVER AND PROCESS at high speed until smooth.
REMOVE feeder cap and add nuts.
CONTINUE TO PROCESS only until nuts are chopped.
ADD to dry ingredients and mix well.
TURN into prepared pan.
BAKE 40 to 50 minutes.
MAKES: one 9-inch cake.

PUMPKIN PIE

2 eggs
1-2/3 cups evaporated milk
3/4 cup sugar
1/2 teaspoon salt
1 teaspoon cinnamon
1/2 teaspoon ginger
1/4 teaspoon cloves
1/4 teaspoon nutmeg
1-1/2 cups canned pumpkin
1 9-inch unbaked pie shell
Whipped cream for garnish

Preheat oven to 400° F.
PLACE eggs, evaporated milk, sugar, seasonings and pumpkin in blender container.
COVER AND PROCESS until thoroughly combined.
STOP BLENDER and scrape down sides of container with rubber spatula, if necessary.
TURN into unbaked pie shell.
BAKE 50-60 minutes or until knife inserted in center comes out clean.
SERVE hot or cold, garnished with whipped cream.
MAKES: 6 to 8 servings.

NO-COOK LEMON PIE

2 eggs, separated
1 can (15 ounces) sweetened condensed milk
1/2 cup lemon juice
Rind from 1 lemon, cut in wedges
1 8-inch baked pie crust, cooled

Preheat oven to 325° F.
PLACE egg yolks, milk, lemon juice and lemon rind in blender container.
COVER AND PROCESS until thickened.
STOP BLENDER and scrape down sides of container with rubber spatula, if necessary.
TURN into cooled pie crust.
CHILL.

Meringue

- Egg whites from eggs, above
- 1/4 cup sugar
- 1/4 teaspoon cream of tartar

WHIP egg whites and cream of tarter until soft peaks form.
GRADUALLY ADD sugar.
BEAT until mixture holds in firm peaks.
PILE onto filling and seal edges.
BAKE 15 minutes or until meringue is golden brown.
CHILL before serving.
MAKES: 6 servings.

CREAM CHEESE PIE

- 16 graham crackers
- 1/2 cup sugar
- 1/4 cup melted butter
- 2 eggs
- Rind of 1 lemon
- 1/8 teaspoon salt
- 3/4 cup sugar
- 4 3-ounce packages cream cheese, softened to room temperature

Preheat oven to 350° F.
BREAK half of crackers into blender container.
COVER AND PROCESS to crumb.
EMPTY into bowl.
REPEAT with remaining crackers.
ADD 1/2 cup sugar and butter to crumbs.
MIX lightly until moistened.
PRESS into 9-inch pie pan.
PLACE eggs, lemon rind, salt and 3/4 cup sugar in blender container.
BREAK softened cream cheese in pieces and add to mixture in blender container.
COVER AND PROCESS on high speed until smooth.
STOP BLENDER and scrape down sides of container with rubber spatula, if necessary.
TURN mixture into pie shell.

BAKE 40 to 60 minutes or until firm.
MAKES: 8 servings.

CHOCOLATE CHIFFON PIE

1 package (6 ounces) semi-sweet chocolate pieces
1/3 cup sugar
1/3 cup very hot water
1 teaspoon vanilla
4 eggs, separated
1 9-inch baked pie crust

PLACE chocolate, sugar, water and vanilla in blender container.
COVER AND PROCESS until smooth. With blender continuing to run,
REMOVE feeder cap and slowly add egg yolks.
INCREASE to high speed and process about 60 seconds until thick.
BEAT egg whites until stiff peaks form.
CAREFULLY FOLD chocolate mixture into egg whites with wire whisk or rubber spatula.
FOLD only until combined.
TURN into baked pie shell.
REFRIGERATE until firm.
MAKES: 8 servings.

COTTAGE CHEESE PIE WITH CRANBERRY GLAZE

1 graham cracker crust
2 tablespoons lemon juice
2 egg yolks
1 envelope unflavored gelatine
1/4 cup hot milk
1/3 cup sugar
2 cups creamed cottage cheese

Prepare graham cracker crust.
PLACE lemon juice, egg yolks and gelatine in blender container.
COVER AND PROCESS as for gelatine.
REMOVE feeder cap and gradually pour in hot milk and sugar.

REPLACE feeder cap and continue processing until gelatine dissolves.
TURN control to high.
REMOVE cover and gradually add cottage cheese.
COVER AND PROCESS until smooth and well blended.
POUR into prepared crust. Chill until set.

Cranberry Glaze

1-1/2 cups fresh cranberries
1/2 cup sugar
2/3 cup orange juice
Thin rind from 1/4 orange

PLACE half of cranberries in blender container.
COVER AND PROCESS until chopped.
EMPTY into saucepan.
REPEAT with remaining berries.
PLACE remaining ingredients in blender container.
COVER AND PROCESS at high speed until rind is chopped.
EMPTY into saucepan with berries.
COOK until cranberries are soft (about 10 minutes).
COOL and spread over cheese pie.
CHILL before serving.
MAKES: 6 to 8 servings.

COTTAGE CHEESE PIE

2 tablespoons cold water
2 tablespoons lemon juice
1 envelope unflavored gelatine
1/2 cup milk, heated to boiling
2 egg yolks
1/3 cup sugar
2 cups creamed cottage cheese (mild, not tangy)
Prepared graham cracker crust
Canned fruit, drained well
Whipped cream for garnish

PLACE cold water, lemon juice and gelatine in blender container.

COVER AND PROCESS at proper speed for gelatine (low) until gelatine is softened.
REMOVE feeder cap from blender container and add boiling milk. If gelatine granules cling to container, use a rubber spatula to push them into the mixture. When gelatine is dissolved,
TURN control so ingredients will liquefy.
ADD egg yolks, sugar, and cottage cheese and continue to process until smooth.
TURN into prepared crust.
CHILL until set, about 2 hours.
TOP with fruit and garnish with whipped cream if desired.
MAKES: 6 to 8 servings.

PINEAPPLE CHEESE PIE

1 envelope unflavored gelatine
1/4 cup cold milk
1/2 cup milk, heated to boiling
2/3 cup sugar
1/8 teaspoon salt
1 package (8 ounces) cream cheese, cut in pieces
1 tablespoon lemon juice
1 cup heavy cream
1 can (8-3/4 ounces) crushed pineapple
1 9-inch crumb crust

SPRINKLE gelatine over cold milk in blender container. Allow to stand while assembling remaining ingredients.
ADD boiling milk to blender container.
COVER AND PROCESS at proper speed for gelatine (low) until gelatine dissolves. If gelatine granules cling to container, use rubber spatula to push them into the mixture. When gelatine is dissolved,
TURN control to highest speed.
ADD sugar, salt, cream cheese, lemon juice and heavy cream.
PROCESS until smooth.
STOP blender.
ADD pineapple and syrup.
TURN blender on and off quickly to stir in pineapple.

TURN into crumb crust.
CHILL until firm, about 3 hours.
MAKES: 6 to 8 servings.

MINCEMEAT CHIFFON PIE

1 envelope unflavored gelatine
1/4 cup cold water
1/2 cup boiling water
1-1/3 cups mincemeat (one-half 28-ounce jar)
1/2 cup cold water
1 tablespoon lemon juice
1/2 cup instant nonfat dry milk, (dry form)
1 9-inch baked pastry crust cooled or graham-cracker crumb crust

SPRINKLE gelatine over 1/4 cup cold water in blender container.
COVER AND PROCESS at proper speed for gelatine (low) until gelatine dissolves.
ADD 1/2 cup boiling water.
COVER AND PROCESS until mixture is foamy.
ADD mincemeat to blender container.
COVER AND PROCESS at low speed until mixture is smooth.
SET ASIDE.
COMBINE 1/2 cup cold water, lemon juice and nonfat dry milk in small mixing bowl.
BEAT at high speed in electric mixer about 6 minutes or until stiff.
POUR mincemeat-gelatine mixture into deep mixing bowl.
PLACE bowl over ice water.
STIR until mixture is cooled and mounds slightly when dropped from a spoon.
REMOVE bowl from ice water.
FOLD whipped nonfat dry milk into cooled mincemeat-gelatine mixture.
TURN into crust.
CHILL in refrigerator 2-3 hours, or until set.
MAKES: 6 to 8 servings.

LEMON PIE

Crust

1 cup matzo meal
1/4 cup shortening
1/2 teaspoon salt
1/2 teaspoon cinnamon
1 teaspoon sugar

Preheat oven to 375° F.
COMBINE the ingredients for the crust in the order given and pat evenly into a 9-inch pie pan.
BAKE 10 minutes or until lightly browned.

Filling

Thinly peeled rind of 1 lemon
2 lemons, peeled, seeded and quartered
1/2 cup sugar
1-1/2 cups water
4 egg yolks
1/2 cup sugar
3 tablespoons potato flour
1/2 cup cold water
4 egg whites beaten stiff with a pinch of salt

PLACE the first 4 ingredients in blender container.
COVER AND PROCESS to liquefy lemons and grate rind.
POUR into saucepan and bring to a boil.
PLACE next 4 ingredients in blender container.
COVER AND PROCESS and add to the boiling ingredients.
STIR over medium heat until thick and smooth.
REMOVE from heat.
LET cool 10 minutes.
STIR into beaten egg whites.
TURN into cooled pie crust.
CHILL before serving.
MAKES: 6 to 8 servings.

MINCEMEAT COOKIES

1-1/2 cups sifted flour
1-1/2 teaspoons baking soda
1/4 cup water
2 eggs
1/3 cup shortening
3/4 cup brown sugar
1/2 teaspoon cinnamon
1/4 teaspoon nutmeg
1/4 teaspoon salt
1/2 cup nuts
1/2 cup packaged mincemeat

Preheat oven to 375° F.
GREASE cookie sheets.
SIFT flour and baking soda together in mixing bowl.
PLACE water, eggs, shortening, sugar, spices and salt in blender container.
COVER AND PROCESS at high speed until smooth.
REMOVE cover and add nuts and mincemeat, continuing to process only until nuts are chopped.
POUR mixture into dry ingredients and mix well.
DROP by teaspoonfuls onto cookie sheet.
BAKE 8 to 10 minutes.
REMOVE from cookie sheet immediately after removing from oven.
MAKES: about 5 dozen.

BITTERSWEET BROWNIES

1-1/2 cups pecans
1/2 cup flour
1 teaspoon baking powder
1/2 teaspoon salt
2 eggs
1/2 cup soft butter
1 cup sugar
1 teaspoon vanilla extract
2 squares unsweetened chocolate, melted

Preheat oven to 350° F. Grease a 9-inch pan.
PLACE pecans in blender container.
COVER AND PROCESS as for nuts.
EMPTY on waxed paper.
SIFT flour, baking powder and salt on waxed paper and set aside.

PLACE eggs, butter, sugar and vanilla in blender container.
COVER AND PROCESS at high speed until smooth.
REMOVE feeder cap and add melted chocolate.
COVER AND PROCESS until smooth.
ADD flour mixture gradually through feeder cap.
STOP BLENDER and add nuts.
MIX into batter with rubber spatula.
SPREAD in prepared pan.
BAKE 20 to 30 minutes or until cake tests done.
COOL AND FROST with Bittersweet Chocolate Frosting.*

**Bittersweet Chocolate Frosting*

- 2 squares unsweetened chocolate, cut in small pieces
- 2 tablespoons butter
- 4 tablespoons hot milk
- 1 cup powdered sugar
- 1 teaspoon vanilla

PLACE all ingredients in blender container.
COVER AND PROCESS until completely smooth. If frosting is too thick add a small amount of cream.
SPREAD over brownies.
COOL.
CUT in 1-1/2-inch squares.

SHORT ALMOND COOKIES

- 1/3 cup whole blanched almonds
- 3/4 cup butter or margarine
- 1/3 cup sugar
- 4 egg yolks
- 2 cups sifted all-purpose flour
- 1/2 teaspoon salt
- 1/2 to 3/4 teaspoon almond extract

Preheat oven to 375° F.
PROCESS almonds in blender container to grind.
CREAM butter and sugar together in mixing bowl.
ADD egg yolks and beat thoroughly.

COMBINE flour and salt and blend into creamed mixture a little at a time.
MIX in almonds and extract.
ROLL on lightly floured surface to 1/4-inch thickness.
CUT into 2x1-inch strips.
BAKE on ungreased cooky sheet 10 to 12 minutes or until lightly browned.
MAKES: 5 to 6 dozen.

ALMOND CRISPIES

1/2 cup whole almonds
1/2 cup butter or margarine
1 cup brown sugar, packed
2 eggs
1/2 cup sifted all-purpose flour
1 teaspoon baking powder
1/4 teaspoon salt
1 teaspoon cinnamon
3/4 cup fine dry bread crumbs
1/4 cup fresh dates, finely cut

Preheat oven to 350° F.
PROCESS almonds in blender container to grind.
CREAM butter and sugar thoroughly in mixing bowl.
ADD eggs.
BEAT well.
SIFT flour with baking powder, salt and cinnamon.
ADD to creamed mixture and blend well.
STIR in almonds, crumbs and dates.
DROP by small spoonfuls onto ungreased cooky sheet about 3 inches apart.
BAKE 12 to 15 minutes.
MAKES: about 4 dozen.

GINGERBREAD

- 1-1/2 cups sifted flour
- 1/4 teaspoon baking soda
- 1-1/2 teaspoons ginger
- 1-1/2 teaspoons cinnamon
- 1/2 teaspoon cloves
- 1/4 teaspoon salt
- 2 eggs
- 1/2 cup molasses
- 1/2 cup sour milk or buttermilk
- 1/2 cup butter or shortening
- 1/2 cup sugar

Preheat oven to 350° F.
GREASE and lightly flour an 8-inch square pan.
SIFT flour, baking soda and spices in mixing bowl.
PLACE remaining ingredients in blender container.
COVER AND PROCESS at high speed until smooth.
STOP BLENDER and scrape down sides of container with rubber spatula, if necessary.
POUR mixture over dry ingredients and mix well.
TURN into prepared pan.
BAKE 20 to 30 minutes or until cake tests done.
MAKES: 9 servings.

PINEAPPLE CHEESE SOUFFLE

1/4 cup dairy sour cream
2 cups Hawaiian pineapple creamed cottage cheese
1/3 cup flour
Dash salt
6 tablespoons sugar, divided
1-1/2 teaspoons lemon juice
3 egg yolks, well beaten
4 egg whites
Pineapple Sauce*

Preheat oven to 300° F.
PLACE sour cream in blender container.
ADD cottage cheese, a half cup at a time.
PROCESS until smooth.
ADD flour and process until smooth.
BEAT salt, 4 tablespoons sugar and lemon juice into egg yolks in mixing bowl.
COMBINE sour cream-cheese mixture and yolk mixture well.
BEAT egg whites until soft peaks form.
ADD 2 tablespoons sugar, one tablespoon at a time.
CONTINUE TO BEAT until whites are stiff but not dry.
FOLD whites into rest of mixture.
TURN into 6-cup, 3-1/4-inch-deep baking dish.
BAKE 1 hour 20 minutes or until firm.
SERVE at once with chilled pineapple sauce.*
MAKES: 6 servings.

**Pineapple Sauce*

2 teaspoons cornstarch
6 tablespoons canned pineapple syrup
6 tablespoons cold water
1/4 cup light corn syrup
1/4 teaspoon lemon juice
Yellow food coloring
2/3 cup chilled, canned, well-drained pineapple tidbits

COMBINE cornstarch, pineapple syrup, water, corn syrup and lemon juice in saucepan.

COOK over medium heat, stirring constantly until sauce thickens slightly.
REMOVE from heat.
STIR in few drops of food coloring.
REFRIGERATE.
ADD pineapple tidbits just before serving.
POUR over pineapple cheese souffle.
MAKES: 1-1/2 cups.

CHOCOLATE CREAM

2 envelopes unflavored gelatine
1/2 cup cold milk
3/4 cup sugar
1/3 cup cocoa
1 cup milk
1 egg
1/8 teaspoon salt
1 teaspoon vanilla
1 cup heavy cream
1 1/2 cups crushed ice
Whipped cream, almonds, chocolate curls

SPRINKLE gelatine over cold milk in blender container.
COVER AND PROCESS at proper speed for gelatine (low) until gelatine is softened.
MIX sugar and cocoa in saucepan.
STIR in milk.
BRING to a boil, stirring constantly.
REMOVE feeder cap from blender container and add hot cocoa mixture.
PROCESS at highest speed until gelatine dissolves.
ADD egg, salt, vanilla, cream and ice.
PROCESS to liquefy.
TURN at once into serving bowl. Allow to set 5 minutes before serving.
GARNISH with additional whipped cream, toasted slivered almonds and chocolate curls.
MAKES: 8 servings.

MINCEMEAT CREME

2 envelopes unflavored gelatine
1/2 cup cold milk
1/2 cup milk, heated to boiling
2 eggs
1/2 orange, cut in pieces and seeded
1/3 cup sugar
1 cup heavy cream
1 cup ice cubes or crushed ice
1-1/2 cups prepared mincemeat

SPRINKLE gelatine over cold milk in blender container. Allow to stand while assembling remaining ingredients.
COVER AND PROCESS at proper speed for gelatine (low) until gelatine is softened.
ADD boiling milk and continue to process until gelatine dissolves. If gelatine granules cling to container, use rubber spatula to push them into the mixture.
ADD eggs, orange and sugar.
COVER AND PROCESS until orange is very finely chopped.
ADD heavy cream and ice cubes one at a time.
PROCESS as for ice cubes until melted.
ADD mincemeat and process until mincemeat is chopped.
TURN into 5-cup mold and chill until firm.
MAKES: 8 servings.
Note: for pie filling, chill mixture until it mounds slightly when dropped from a spoon. Turn into 9-inch baked pastry shell or crumb crust and chill until firm.

ORANGE SPANISH CREAM

1 envelope unflavored gelatine
1/4 cup cold milk
1-3/4 cup milk, heated to boiling
1/2 cup sugar, divided
1/4 teaspoon salt
1/2 teaspoon vanilla
2 eggs, separated
Rind of one orange (remove in thin strips with vegetable peeler)

SPRINKLE gelatine over cold milk in blender container. Allow to stand while assembling remaining ingredients.
ADD boiling milk.
COVER AND PROCESS at proper speed for gelatine (low) until gelatine dissolves. If gelatine granules cling to container, use a rubber spatula to push them into the mixture. When gelatine is dissolved,
ADD 1/4 cup of sugar, salt, vanilla, egg yolks and orange rind.
COVER AND PROCESS to liquefy and until rind is in very tiny pieces.
CHILL, stirring occasionally, until mixture mounds slightly when dropped from a spoon.
BEAT egg whites until stiff, but not dry.
GRADUALLY ADD remaining 1/4 cup sugar and beat until very stiff.
FOLD in chilled orange mixture.
TURN into individual serving dishes.
CHILL and firm, about 2 to 3 hours.
MAKES: 6 servings.

MINT CREAM

- 2 envelopes unflavored gelatin
- 2-1/2 cups milk, divided
- 2 eggs
- 2/3 cup sugar
- 1/8 teaspoon salt
- 1/4 cup green creme de menthe
- 1 cup heavy cream
- Sprigs of mint for garnish

SPRINKLE gelatine over 1/2 cup milk in blender container. Allow to soften while assembling remaining ingredients.
BRING one cup milk to full boil.
POUR into blender container.
COVER AND PROCESS at low speed for 10 seconds and high for 20 seconds.
ADD remaining 1 cup milk, eggs, sugar, salt and green creme de menthe.
COVER AND PROCESS at high speed for 15 seconds.
TURN into mixing bowl and stir in cream.
TURN into 5-cup mold, bowl or individual serving dishes.
CHILL until firm, about 3 hours.
GARNISH with sprigs of mint, if desired.
MAKES: 8 servings.

PRONTO PRUNE WHIP

- 1 envelope unflavored gelatine
- 1/4 cup lemon juice
- 1/2 cup boiling prune liquid or prune juice
- 1/2 cup sugar
- 1 cup heavy cream
- 1/2 cup (about 5) ice cubes
- 1 cup cooked whole pitted prunes
- Whipped cream for garnish

SPRINKLE gelatine over lemon juice in blender container.
ADD boiling prune liquid.
COVER AND PROCESS at proper speed for gelatine (low) until gelatine dissolves.
ADD sugar, cream and ice cubes one at a time and process as for ice cubes until melted.

ADD prunes and process as for fuit until prunes are chopped.
TURN into serving dishes.
CHILL about 1 hour.
GARNISH with additional whipped cream and top with additional prunes, if desired.
MAKES: 4 to 6 servings.

LEMON CREAM

1 envelope unflavored gelatine
1/4 cup lemon juice
Rind of 1 lemon (remove rind in thin strips with vegetable peeler)
1/2 cup boiling water
2 eggs
1 cup sugar
1/8 teaspoon salt
1 cup heavy cream

SPRINKLE gelatine over lemon juice in blender container. Allow to stand while assembling remaining ingredients.
ADD lemon rind and boiling water.
COVER AND PROCESS at proper speed for gelatine (low) until gelatine dissolves and lemon rind is in very tiny pieces. If gelatine granules cling to container, use a rubber spatula to push them into the mixture. When gelatine is dissolved,
ADD remaining ingredients and process at high speed until smooth and well blended.
TURN into 3-cup mold, bowl or individual serving dishes.
CHILL until firm, about 3 hours.
SERVE with Apricot Sauce.*
MAKES: 6 servings.

**Apricot Sauce*

1 can (1 pound) apricot halves
2 tablespoons apricot liqueur

DRAIN apricots and reserve syrup.
PLACE apricots, 1/4 cup apricot syrup and liqueur in blender container.

COVER AND PROCESS as for fruits until liquefied and smooth.
MAKES: 1 cup.

PEACH MELBA MOLD

2 envelopes unflavored gelatine
1/2 cup cold milk
1 cup milk, heated to boiling
1/2 lemon, peeled and seeded
1/2 cup sugar
1/8 teaspoon salt
1 package (12 ounces) frozen peaches, thawed
1 cup heavy cream
1 cup ice cubes or crushed ice

SPRINKLE gelatine over cold milk in blender container that will hold 5 cups. Allow to stand while assembling remaining ingredients.
ADD boiling milk.
COVER AND PROCESS at proper speed for gelatine (low) until gelatine dissolves.
ADD lemon, sugar, salt, peaches and cream.
COVER AND PROCESS at high speed until smooth.
ADD ice cubes one at a time.
PROCESS as for ice cubes until melted.
TURN into 5-cup mold, bowl or individual serving dishes.
CHILL until firm, about 2-3 hours.
UNMOLD and serve with Melba Sauce.*
Makes: 6 servings.
Note: If blender container will not hold 5 cups, do not add cream to blender. After ice cubes are melted, quickly pour gelatine mixture into a bowl and beat in cream.

**Melba Sauce*

1 package 10 ounces) frozen raspberries, thawed

PLACE raspberries in blender container.
COVER AND PROCESS to a purée.
STRAIN.
MAKES: 3/4 cup.

CHOCOLATE RUM PARFAITS

2 envelopes unflavored gelatine
1/4 cup cold milk
6 tablespoons dark rum
3/4 cup milk, heated to boiling
1 egg
1/4 cup sugar
1/8 teaspoon salt
1 6-ounce package (1 cup) semi-sweet chocolate pieces
2 cups heavy cream, divided
1-1/2 cups ice cubes or crushed ice
1 teaspoon vanilla
1/2 cup chopped toasted pecans

SPRINKLE gelatine over milk and rum in blender container. Allow to stand while assembling other ingredients.
ADD boiling milk.
COVER AND PROCESS at proper speed for gelatine (low) until gelatine dissolves. If gelatine granules cling to container, use a rubber spatula to push them into the mixture.
ADD egg, sugar and salt.
TURN control to high speed.
ADD chocolate and process until smooth.
ADD 1 cup cream.
ADD ice cubes one at a time and process as for ice cubes until melted.
LET STAND 15 minutes to thicken.
ADD vanilla to remaining 1 cup cream and whip until stiff.
ALTERNATE chocolate mixture, whipped cream and chopped pecans in parfait glasses. Serve immediately or chill.
MAKES: 8 servings.

BROADWAY BAVARIANS

Vanilla layer:

1 envelope unflavored gelatine
1/4 cup cold milk
1/2 cup milk, heated to boiling
1 egg
1/4 cup sugar
1/8 teaspoon salt
1 teaspoon vanilla
1/2 cup heavy cream
3/4 cup ice cubes or crushed ice

SPRINKLE gelatine over cold milk in blender container.
COVER AND PROCESS at proper speed for gelatine (low) until gelatine is softened.
REMOVE feeder cap from blender container and add boiling milk.
CONTINUE TO PROCESS until gelatine dissolves. If gelatine granules cling to container, use a rubber spatula to push them into the mixture. When gelatine is dissolved,
ADD egg, sugar, salt and vanilla.
COVER AND PROCESS to whip.
ADD cream, then ice cubes one at a time.
PROCESS as for ice cubes until melted.
POUR immediately into six 8-ounce glasses or eight 6-ounce glasses.
Rinse blender container and prepare chocolate layer.

Chocolate layer:

1 envelope unflavored gelatine
1/4 cup cold milk
1/2 cup milk, heated to boiling
1 egg
2 tablespoons sugar
1/8 teaspoon salt
1/2 cup semi-sweet chocolate pieces
1/2 teaspoon vanilla
1/2 cup heavy cream
3/4 cup ice cubes or crushed ice

SPRINKLE gelatine over cold milk into blender container.

COVER AND PROCESS at proper speed for gelatin (low) until gelatin is softened.
REMOVE feeder cap from blender container and add boiling milk.
COVER AND PROCESS until gelatine dissolves. If gelatine granules cling to container, use a rubber spatula to push them into the mixture. When gelatine is dissolved,
ADD egg, sugar and salt.
ADD chocolate pieces and process at highest speed until smooth.
ADD vanilla, cream and ice cubes one at a time.
PROCESS as for ice cubes until melted.
POUR at once over vanilla layer in glasses. Allow to set 15 minutes before serving.
GARNISH with additional whipped cream, if desired.
MAKES: 5 to 8 servings.

CHERRY WHIRL

2 envelopes unflavored gelatine
1/4 cup maraschino cherry syrup
1/4 cup cold pineapple juice
1/2 cup boiling pineapple juice
1/2 cup maraschino cherries
1/2 lemon, peeled and seeded
1/3 cup sugar
1/2 cup light cream
2 cups crushed ice or ice cubes
Whipped cream and cherries for garnish

SPRINKLE gelatine over cherry syrup and cold pineapple juice in blender container. Allow to stand while assembling remaining ingredients.
ADD boiling pineapple juice.
COVER AND PROCESS at proper speed for gelatine (low) until gelatine dissolves. If gelatine granules cling to container, use a rubber spatula to push them into the mixture. When gelatine is dissolved,
TURN to highest speed.

ADD cherries, lemon, sugar, cream and ice cubes, one at a time.
PROCESS until ice is melted and mixture begins to thicken.
POUR at once into 5-cup mold, bowl or individual serving dishes.
CHILL mold about 1 hour.
CHILL individual servings 5 minutes.
GARNISH with additional whipped cream and cherries.
MAKES: 6 to 8 servings.

ALMOND CHOCOLATE BALLS

3/4 cup whole blanched almonds
1/4 cup honey
1 tablespoon soft butter or margarine
1/4 teaspoon almond extract
Dash salt
4 ounces semi-sweet candy-making chocolate

PROCESS almonds in blender container to grind.
MIX almonds, honey, butter, almond extract and salt together in mixing bowl.
FORM into 1-inch balls.
CUT chocolate into small pieces.
MELT over hot (not boiling) water, stirring until smooth.
DIP balls in chocolate.
PLACE on waxed paper to harden.
MAKES: 2 dozen.

CHOCOLATE MINI-MOUSSE

1/4 cup cold water
2 envelopes unflavored gelatine
3/4 cup boiling water
1/3 cup instant nonfat dry milk (dry form)
1/4 cup sugar
1 package (6 ounces) semi-sweet chocolate pieces
2 cups crushed ice

SPRINKLE gelatine over cold water in blender container.
PROCESS at proper speed for gelatine (low) until gelatine is softened.
ADD boiling water.
COVER AND PROCESS until gelatine dissolves.
ADD nonfat dry milk, sugar and chocolate pieces.
PROCESS at high speed until chips are melted.
ADD crushed ice and process until mixture begins to thicken, about 1 minute.
POUR immediately into dessert dishes.
MAKES: 4 servings.

CHOCOLATE MOUSSE

2 envelopes unflavored gelatine
1/2 cup cold milk
3/4 cup milk, heated to boiling
1 egg
1/4 cup sugar
1/8 teaspoon salt
1 teaspoon vanilla
1 6-ounce package (1 cup) semi-sweet chocolate pieces
1 cup heavy cream
1-1/2 cups ice cubes or crushed ice

SPRINKLE gelatine over cold milk in blender container that will hold 5 cups. Allow to stand while assembling remaining ingredients.
ADD boiling milk.
COVER AND PROCESS at proper speed for gelatine (low) until gelatine dissolves.

ADD egg, sugar, salt, vanilla and chocolate pieces.
COVER AND PROCESS at high speed until smooth.
ADD cream and ice cubes, one at a time.
PROCESS as for ice cubes until melted.
TURN at once into 5-cup mold, bowl or individual serving dishes.
CHILL about 1 hour.
CHILL individual servings 15 minutes.
MAKES: 8 servings.
Note: If blender container will not hold 5 cups, do not add cream to blender. After ice cubes are melted, quickly pour gelatine mixture into a bowl and beat in cream.

APRICOT MOUSSE

(Recipe to be made twice for 10-cup mold)

2 envelopes unflavored gelatine
1 can (1 pound, 14 ounces) apricot halves
1 egg
1/4 cup sugar
1/8 teaspoon salt
1-1/2 tablespoons lemon juice
1 cup heavy cream
Whipped cream for garnish
Candied violets or small gumdrops for garnish

SPRINKLE gelatine over 1/2 cup apricot syrup in blender container that will hold 5 cups.
BRING remaining syrup to a boil.
ADD to container.
COVER AND PROCESS at proper speed for gelatine (low) until gelatine dissolves. When gelatine is dissolved,
ADD drained apricots, egg, sugar, salt, lemon juice and heavy cream.
COVER AND PROCESS at high speed until blended.
TURN into a 10-cup melon mold or two 5-cup molds.
REPEAT recipe and add to mold.
CHILL 8 hours or overnight, until firm.
UNMOLD.

GARNISH with whipped cream and candied violets or small gumdrops.
MAKES: 12 to 16 servings.
Note: If blender container will not hold 5-cup volume, do not add cream with other ingredients. Turn mixture into bowl and stir in cream, then pour into mold.

RASPBERRY MACAROON MOUSSE

2 packages frozen raspberries, thawed
2 cups heavy cream
2 egg whites
1/2 cup sugar
2/3 cup crisp macaroon crumbs

PLACE raspberries in blender container.
COVER AND PROCESS until puréed.
STRAIN AND POUR into mixing bowl.
PLACE cream into chilled blender container.
COVER AND BEAT at low speed.
REMOVE and fold into raspberries.
BEAT egg whites with rotary beater, gradually adding sugar.
CONTINUE BEATING until stiff but not dry.
FOLD into cream mixture.
SPOON into 2-quart mold.
PLACE in freezer 1 hour.
PLACE few macaroon cookies in blender container.
COVER AND PROCESS until 2/3 cup crumbs are produced.
COVER mousse with crumbs.
SWIRL with knife to form streaks.
CONTINUE freezing until firm.
MAKES: 6 servings.

CHERRY-BERRY DESSERT

1 envelope unflavored gelatine
1/4 cup cold water
1 cup cranberry juice, heated to boilng
1/4 cup sugar
1/8 teaspoon salt
1 can (8-3/4 ounces) pitted dark sweet cherries
2 teaspoons lemon juice
Whipped cream for garnish

SPRINKLE gelatine over cold water in blender container. Allow to stand while assembling remaining ingredients.
ADD cranberry juice.
COVER AND PROCESS at proper speed for gelatine (low) until gelatine dissolves. If gelatine granules cling to container, use a rubber spatula to push them into the mixture.
ADD remaining ingredients.
COVER AND PROCESS as for fruits until cherries are in fine peices.
TURN into 3-cup mold or individual serving dishes.
CHILL until firm, about 2 to 3 hours.
GARNISH with whipped cream if desired.
MAKES: 4 to 6 servings.

JIFFY GELATINE DESSERT

1 package (3 ounces) raspberry flavored gelatin
Granulated sugar
1/2 cup very hot water
8 to 10 ice cubes
1 package frozen raspberries, thawed
Raspberries for garnish

DIP rims of sherbet dishes into raspberry juice from thawed berries, then into sugar. Put dishes into refrigerator to chill.
PLACE gelatin and water in blender container.
COVER AND PROCESS until gelatin is dissolved.
STOP BLENDER and scrape down sides of container with rubber spatula, if necessary.

INCREASE to high speed. With blender continuing to run,
REMOVE feeder cap and slowly add ice cubes one at a time.
PROCESS at correct speed for ice cubes.
POUR immediately into chilled sherbet dishes, leaving about one-half inch between frosted rim and gelatin mixture.
REFRIGERATE 3 to 5 minutes or until set.
GARNISH with raspberries.
MAKES: 6 servings.

RASPBERRY BAVARIAN

1 cup boiling water
1 package (3 ounces) raspberry flavored gelatin
1 envelope unflavored gelatine
1 can (6 ounces) frozen orange juice concentrate, thawed
1/2 cup cold water
1 pint vanilla ice cream

PLACE boiling water, raspberry and unflavored gelatine in blender container.
COVER AND PROCESS on low until gelatine dissolves.
ADD orange juice and cold water.
COVER AND PROCESS until completely combined.
ADD ice cream.
COVER AND PROCESS until thoroughly blended.
STOP BLENDER and scrape down sides of container with rubber spatula, if necessary.
TURN immediately into a 1-1/2-quart mold.
REFRIGERATE until very firm. Unmold to serve.
MAKES: 6 servings.

PINK APPLESAUCE

6 medium-sized tart apples, peeled, cored, quartered
1 wedge lemon
1/4 cup water
1/4 cup red cinnamon candies
Sugar

PLACE half of apples, lemon wedge, water and cinnamon candies in blender container.
COVER AND PROCESS on high speed until apples are finely chopped. With blender continuing to run, REMOVE feeder cap and slowly add remaining apples.
COVER AND PROCESS until apples are finely chopped.
ADD sugar to taste.
REFRIGERATE until serving.
MAKES: 3 cups.

CARAMEL FLAN

1-3/4 cups sugar, divided
8 eggs
3-1/3 cups evaporated milk
2 teaspoons vanilla

Preheat oven to 350° F.
PLACE 1 cup sugar into an 8-inch square pan in which the custard is to be baked.
COOK, stirring constantly, over medium heat until sugar melts and is light amber.
TIP the pan around until it is entirely coated with the caramel mixture.
COOL.
PLACE eggs, milk, remaining sugar and vanilla into blender container.
COVER AND PROCESS until well mixed.
TURN into caramel-coated pan.
COVER and place in a larger pan.
POUR in 1 inch of hot water.

BAKE 1 hour or until knife inserted near edge of custard comes out clean.
UNMOLD immediately.
MAKES: 9 servings.

PINEAPPLE-MINT FREEZE

1 can (13 ounces) frozen pineapple chunks
1-1/2 ounces crème de menthe

PLACE ingredients in blender container.
COVER AND PROCESS on high speed until mixture is of a sherbet consistency.
STOP BLENDER and scrape down sides of container with rubber spatula if necessary.
CHILL.
SERVE in chilled sherbet dishes.
MAKES: 2 servings.

FROZEN LIME CREME

Juice of 2 limes
1-1/2 cups orange juice
1 pound marshmallows
Few drops of green food coloring
3 cups heavy cream
Thin lime slices for garnish

PLACE juices and 6 marshmallows in blender container.
COVER AND PROCESS at high speed until smooth.
REMOVE feeder cap and add remaining marshmallows, one at a time. When smooth,
ADD food coloring.
REPLACE feeder cap and process to blend.
POUR into medium-size mixing bowl.
REFRIGERATE until mixture begins to thicken slightly.
POUR cream into blender container.
COVER AND PROCESS at low speed until whipped.
FOLD cream into chilled mixture.

TURN into 6-cup mold and freeze 3 to 4 hours or overnight.
ONE-HALF HOUR BEFORE SERVING, REMOVE from freezer and let stand at room temperature.
UNMOLD on serving dish.
GARNISH with thin lime slices.
MAKES: 6 to 8 servings.

BANANA ICE CREAM

3 medium bananas, fully ripe
1/2 cup orange juice
2 to 3 drops yellow food coloring
12 marshmallows
1 cup whipping cream

PLACE all ingredients except whipping cream in blender container.
COVER AND PROCESS until smooth.
STOP BLENDER and scrape down sides of container with rubber spatula, if necessary.
WHIP cream until stiff.
FOLD in banana mixture.
TURN into refrigerator tray.
FREEZE until firm.
MAKES: one tray ice cream.

BLACKBERRY ICE CREAM

1 can (1 pound, 5 ounces) blackberry pie filling
1 tablespoon lemon juice
1 cup whipping cream
1 cup powdered sugar

PLACE pie filling and lemon juice in blender container.
COVER AND PROCESS at medium speed until smooth.
STOP BLENDER and scrape down sides of container with rubber spatula if necessary.
WHIP cream until it holds a soft peak.
ADD powdered sugar and beat until stiff.

FOLD in blackberry pie filling.
POUR into two refrigerator trays.
FREEZE until firm.
MAKES: two trays ice cream.
VARIATIONS: Substitute one can (1 pound 5 ounces) blueberry or cherry pie filling.

CINNAMON-APPLE ICE CREAM

1 envelope unflavored gelatine
1/2 cup boiling water
1 can (6 ounces) frozen apple juice (concentrated)
6 ounces cold water
2 tart eating apples, peeled cored, cut in quarters
1 teaspoon lemon juice
1 teaspoon cinnamon
1/2-3/4 cup sugar
1 cup heavy cream

SPRINKLE gelatine into boiling water.
STIR until dissolved.
PLACE gelatine and remaining ingredients, except heavy cream in blender container.
COVER AND PROCESS until apples are chopped.
STOP BLENDER and scrape down sides of container with rubber spatula, if necessary.
WHIP cream until stiff.
FOLD in gelatine mixture.
POUR into two freezer trays.
FREEZE ABOUT 4 hours until firm.
MAKES: two trays ice cream.

PEACH ICE CREAM

4 to 6 ripe peaches (or 1/2 cup peach purée
1 tablespoon lemon juice
1 cup heavy cream
1 cup confectioners sugar

PEEL peaches and remove pits.
PLACE peaches and lemon juice in blender container.
COVER AND PROCESS to purée.
STOP BLENDER and scrape down sides of container with rubber spatula, if necessary.

WHIP cream until it holds a soft peak.
ADD powdered sugar and continue to beat until stiff.
FOLD in peach purée.
TURN into refrigerator trays.
FREEZE approximately two to four hours until firm.
MAKES: two trays ice cream.

Dessert Sauces

QUICK BUTTERSCOTCH SAUCE

1/2 cup light cream
1-1/2 cups granulated brown sugar
2 tablespoons soft butter
1 teaspoon vanilla extract
1/8 teaspoon salt

PLACE all ingredients in blender container.
COVER AND PROCESS at high speed until smooth.
STORE in covered jar in refrigerator.
SERVE over ice cream.
MAKES: 2 cups.

BLENDER BERRY SAUCE

1 package (10 ounces) frozen raspberries or strawberries, thawed
1/2 cup orange juice
1 tablespoon corn starch

COMBINE all ingredients in blender container.
COVER AND PROCESS at high speed until ingredients are well blended, about 1 minute.
POUR into saucepan. Bring to full boil, stirring constantly.
BOIL 1 minute.
SERVE warm over ice cream or cake.
MAKES: 1-1/4 cups.

EASY CHOCOLATE SAUCE

1 package (6 ounces) semi-sweet chocolate pieces
1/4 cup sugar
1/4 cup very hot water

PLACE all ingredients in blender container.
COVER AND PROCESS to grate until smooth.
STOP BLENDER and scrape down sides of container with rubber spatula, if necessary.
MAKES: 1 cup.

CARAMEL SAUCE

3/4 cup brown sugar
2 tablespoons soft butter
1/4 teaspoon salt
1/2 cup hot evaporated milk

PLACE all ingredients in blender container.
COVER AND PROCESS on low speed until sugar is dissolved.
MAKES 1-1/4 cups.

CHOCOLATE SAUCE

2 squares unsweetened chocolate, cut into pieces
1/4 cup sugar
Dash of salt
1/4 cup light corn syrup
1/3 cup hot milk
1/2 teaspoon vanilla extract

PLACE all ingredients in blender container.
COVER AND PROCESS until chocolate is liquefied and sauce is thick and creamy.
MAKES: 3/4 cup.

Drinks

NECTARINE DAIQUIRI

- 1 fresh nectarine, peeled, pitted and diced
- 2 teaspoons sugar
- 2 tablespoons lime juice
- 1/2 cup light rum
- 1 to 1-1/2 cups finely crushed ice

PLACE nectarine, sugar, lime juice and rum in blender container.
COVER AND PROCESS until smooth.
ADD ice and process until frappéed.
SERVE in chilled champagne glasses.
MAKES: 3 to 4 daiquiris.

SILVER FIZZ

- 1 jigger (4 tablespoons) gin
- 1 tablespoon fresh lemon juice
- 1 tablespoon cracked ice
- 1 tablespoon light corn syrup
- 1 egg white

PLACE all ingredients in blender container and process as for beverages until foamy.
SERVE in whiskey sour or parfait glass.
MAKES: 1 serving.

QUEEN OF THE ISLANDS

3/4 cup orange juice
1/4 cup lime juice
2 tablespoons sugar
1 egg white, unbeaten
1 cup sweet white wine
1 cup crushed ice or
4 whole ice cubes

COMBINE juices and sugar in blender container.
COVER AND PROCESS on low speed until sugar is liquefied.
STOP BLENDER.
ADD egg white, wine and ice.
COVER AND PROCESS on high speed only until ice is liquefied.
POUR into cocktail glasses.
MAKES: eight 3-ounce cocktails.

CZARINA'S DELIGHT

2 tablespoons lemon juice
1 cup grape juice
2 tablespoons sugar
2 jiggers vodka
1 egg white, unbeaten
1 cup crushed ice or
4 whole ice cubes

PLACE juices and sugar in blender container.
COVER AND PROCESS on low until sugar is liquefied.
STOP BLENDER.
ADD egg white, vodka and ice.
COVER AND PROCESS on high speed only until ice is liquefied.
POUR into cocktail glasses.
MAKES: six 3-ounce cocktails.

GRASSHOPPER

2 jiggers white crème de cacao
1 jigger crème de menthe
1 jigger heavy cream
3/4 cup crushed ice or 3 whole ice cubes

PLACE all ingredients in blender container.
COVER AND PROCESS at high speed until smooth.
STRAIN into cocktail glasses.
MAKES: two 3-ounce drinks.

ALEXANDER

2 jiggers gin or brandy
1-1/2 jiggers brown crème de cacao
1 jigger heavy cream
3/4 cup crushed ice or 3 whole ice cubes

PLACE all ingredients in blender container.
COVER AND PROCESS at high speed until smooth.
STRAIN into cocktail glasses.
MAKES: two 3-ounce drinks.

ROSE COOL BLOSSOM

1 can (6 ounces) frozen lemonade concentrate, undiluted
1-1/2 cups rosé wine
1 cup crushed ice or 4 whole ice cubes

PLACE all ingredients in blender container.
COVER AND PROCESS at high speed until ice is liquefied.
POUR into cocktail glasses.
MAKES: eight 3-ounce drinks.

ROSE PETAL

- 1/2 pint raspberry sherbet
- 1 jigger brandy
- 1 jigger white crème de cacao
- 1/2 cup crushed ice or 2 whole ice cubes

PLACE all ingredients in blender container.
COVER AND PROCESS at high speed until smooth.
SERVE in cocktail glasses.
MAKES: four 3-ounce drinks.

SIDE CAR

- 1 tablespoon lime juice
- 2 jiggers brandy
- 1 jigger Cointreau
- 1 cup crushed ice or 4 whole ice cubes

PLACE all ingredients in blender container.
COVER AND PROCESS at high speed a few seconds.
STRAIN into cocktail glasses.
MAKES: two 3-ounce drinks.

CRICKET

- 2 jiggers brown crème de cacao
- 1 jigger brandy
- 1/2 pint vanilla ice cream, softened
- 1 cup crushed ice or 4 whole ice cubes

PLACE all ingredients in blender container.
COVER AND PROCESS at high speed until ice is frappéed.
SERVE in cocktail glasses.
MAKES: 2 tall drinks.

KISS O' THE NILE

1/2 pint lemon-lime sherbet
2 jiggers gin
1/2 cup crushed ice or 2 whole ice cubes

PLACE all ingredients in blender container.
COVER AND PROCESS as for ice cubes until smooth.
SERVE in cocktail glasses.
MAKES: four 3-ounce drinks.

STINGER

2 jiggers brandy
1 jigger wine crème de menthe
1 cup crushed ice or 4 whole ice cubes

PLACE all ingredients in blender container.
COVER AND PROCESS at high speed a few seconds.
STRAIN into cocktail glasses.
MAKES: two 3-ounce drinks.

SACK POSSET

3 cups milk
1/2 cup sugar
1 tablespoon flour
1/2 teaspoon nutmeg
2 eggs
1/2 cup sherry

PLACE all ingredients except sherry in blender container.
COVER AND PROCESS at low speed until well blended.
POUR into saucepan and cook over medium heat, stirring constantly, until slightly thickened.
ADD sherry slowly, stirring constantly.
SERVE warm in mugs or punch cups.
MAKES: eight 1/2-cups.

BACARDI

1/3 cup frozen limeade concentrate, thawed
4 jiggers light rum
1-1/2 cups crushed ice or 6 whole ice cubes
3 tablespoons grenadine

PLACE all ingredients in blender container.
COVER AND PROCESS at high speed a few seconds.
STRAIN into cocktail glasses.
MAKES: four 3-ounce drinks.

DAIQUIRI

1/3 cup frozen limeade concentrate, thawed
4 jiggers light rum
1-1/2 cups crushed ice or 6 whole ice cubes

PLACE all ingredients in blender container.
COVER AND PROCESS as for ice cubes, a few seconds.
STRAIN into cockail glasses.
MAKES: four 3-ounce drinks.

APPLE COCKTAIL FLIP

1 can (8 ounces) applesauce
1-1/2 teaspoon rum or brandy extract
3 tablespoons sugar
2-1/4 cups milk
3 small scoops vanilla ice cream
6 crushed ice cubes

COMBINE all ingredients in blender container.
PROCESS as for ice 1 minute or until very frothy.
MAKES: 3 tall drinks.

DUTCH MILK SHAKE

1 cup chocolate drink
1 medium scoop ice cream, vanilla or chocolate
Few grains of salt

COMBINE all ingredients in blender container.
PROCESS just until fluffy and thick.
SERVE with butter cookies.
MAKES: about 1-1/2 cups.

PINK VELVET FROST

1 cup crushed ice
2/3 cup (1 small can) evaporated milk
1/2 cup sugar
1 package (10 ounces) frozen strawberries

PLACE all ingredients in blender container.
BREAK fruit apart with a fork.
PROCESS as for beverages until thick and creamy, about 1-2 minutes.
SERVE immediately as a drink or freeze in ice tray until ready to serve as a dessert.
MAKES: 4 servings.

Miscellaneous

TOMATO-VEGETABLE RELISH

2 envelopes unflavored gelatine
1/2 cup cold tomato juice
1 cup boiling tomato juice
1-1/4 teaspoons salt
1 cup salad dressing
1 tablespoon Worcestershire sauce
1 tablespoon lemon juice
1 cup celery pieces
1 cup carrot pieces
1/2 green pepper, cut in pieces
1/2 cup radishes
Salad greens

SPRINKLE gelatine over cold tomato juice in blender container. Allow to stand while assembling remaining ingredients.
ADD boiling tomato juice.
COVER AND PROCESS at proper speed for gelatine (low) until gelatine dissolves. If gelatine granules cling to the sides of the container, use a rubber spatula to push them into the mixture. When gelatine is dissolved, ADD salt, salad dressing, Worcestershire sauce and lemon juice.
COVER AND PROCESS until smooth.
STOP BLENDER AND ADD celery, carrot, pepper and radishes.
COVER AND PROCESS only until all pieces are coarsely chopped.
TURN into 5-cup mold.
CHILL until firm.
UNMOLD and serve with salad greens.
MAKES: 8 servings.

CRANBERRY RELISH

1/2 cup orange juice
1 unpeeled orange, quartered
2 cups cranberries
1 tart, unpeeled apple, cored, and quartered
1 cup sugar

PLACE half the ingredients except sugar in blender container.
COVER AND PROCESS until chopped to desired consistency.
STOP BLENDER and scrape down sides of container with rubber spatula, if necessary.
EMPTY into a bowl.
REPEAT with remaining ingredients.
STIR in sugar.
COVER AND REFRIGERATE.
MAKES: 3 cups.

APPLE BUTTER

1/2 cup water
1 teaspoon vinegar
3/4 teaspoon cinnamon
Dash salt
1/8 teaspoon cloves
Small piece lemon rind (yellow portion only)
1/2 cup brown sugar
3 large tart apples, cored and cut in 1-inch pieces

PLACE all ingredients except apples in blender container.
ADD half the apples.
COVER AND PROCESS on high speed until smooth.
ADD remaining apples.
COVER AND PROCESS about 15 seconds until smooth.
TURN into a saucepan and cook 30 to 40 minutes until thick.
SEAL in sterilized jars.
MAKES: 1 pint.

CORN RELISH

2 cups vinegar
1 tablespoon dry mustard
1 tablespoon celery seed
1 tablespoon salt
1-1/4 cups light brown sugar, firmly packed
1/4 sweet red pepper, cut in 1-inch pieces
1 small green pepper, cut in 1-inch pieces
1 large onion, cut in 1-inch pieces
4 cups cooked or canned sweet corn, drained

PLACE all ingredients except corn in blender container.
COVER AND PROCESS until vegetables are chopped.
TURN into 3-quart saucepan.
ADD corn.
COOK slowly 20 minutes over medium heat.
SEAl in sterilzed hot jars.
MAKES: 4 pints.

INDEX